Careers in Focus

TITLE ENTRY

Technicians.

Ferguson Publishing Company
Chicago, Illinois

Andrew Morkes, *Managing Editor-Career Publications*
Carol Yehling, *Senior Editor*
Anne Paterson, *Editor*
Nora Walsh, *Editorial Assistant*

Copyright © 2001 Ferguson Publishing Company
ISBN 0-89434-358-0

Library of Congress Cataloging-in-Publication Data

Careers in Focus. Technicians
    p. cm.
  Includes index.
  ISBN 0-89434-358-0
    1. Industrial technicians--Vocational guidance. 2. Technology--Vocational
guidance. [4. Technology--Vocational guidance. 2. Vocational guidance.]
I. Title: Technicians. II. Ferguson Publishing Company.

TA158 .C365 2000
602.3--dc21

                                                              00-039390

Printed in the United States of America

Cover photo courtesy Andrew Errington/Tony Stone Images

Published and distributed by
Ferguson Publishing Company
200 West Jackson Boulevard, 7th Floor
Chicago, Illinois 60606
800-306-9941
www.fergpubco.com

X-8

Table of Contents

Introduction

Technicians are highly specialized workers who work with scientists, physicians, engineers, and other professionals, as well as with clients and customers. They assist these professionals in many activities, assist clients or customers, and they frequently direct skilled workers. They work in factories, businesses, science labs, hospitals, law offices, clinics, shops, and private homes. Some work for themselves as consultants. They are found in all facets of the work world and are one of the fastest growing job ranks.

First and foremost, a technician is a specialist. When looking at the range of job classifications in the traditional, hierarchical sense, the technician is the middleman, between the scientist in the laboratory and the worker on the floor, between the engineer and the factory worker. In short, the technician's realm is where the scientific meets the practical application, where theory meets product.

Little by little, however, industries and businesses are recasting the traditional paradigm. All workers, be they scientist, manager, technician, or line worker, are coming to be viewed as part of a team. Competency and knowledge are the new standards by which workers are valued, not rank alone. Thus technicians are seen by many as valuable employees in their own right, not simply junior scientists or engineers or wannabe doctors. The work they do is normally supportive of their more prestigious professional colleagues; in fact, basic to the definition of technician is their supportive role—their work adds to and enhances the work of someone else. What is often overlooked, however, is that the work of the professionals frequently could not be done without them. Think about it. Would you really want your lawyer spending hours of time in the library researching your case? Or the automotive engineer fixing your car? Of course not. Assuming that the professional could even remember that far back in his or her training to perform the work, it is certain that he or she does not know the technician's specialty as well as the technician. No, the lawyer should be hard at work creating brilliant summations to win cases; the engineer designing more efficient, better cars. The technician's job is to make all of this possible.

One reason for the growing reliance on technicians is our own growing reliance on technology. As businesses switch to automated systems, as products we buy become more technologically complex, technicians are needed to help design, implement, run, and repair such systems or equipment, be they automobiles, airplanes, X-ray machines, or computer networks. Even in areas that aren't themselves obviously "techno," there exists a certain expectation of speed, efficiency, and quality that is frequently the domain of the technician.

Another reason for the ascension of technicians is their overall cost when compared to that of highly paid professionals such as doctors, lawyers, and engineers and scientists. While in some industries technicians work alongside professionals as valued members of the team, contributing their unique knowledge and skills in areas professionals lack the time to fully develop, technicians in other industries are actually replacing professionals because they are cheaper.

In most cases the increasing reliance on technology creates more jobs for technicians. In a few areas, however, technology is actually replacing technicians. Meteorological technicians, for example, are being phased out completely from jobs with the federal government (National Weather Service). Their painstaking instrument readings and weather data collection work can now be done entirely with high tech instruments. Telephone and cable TV line installers and repairers, EKG technicians, and home electronic entertainment equipment repairers are other technician specialties that are in decline because of advances in technology.

Overall, however, the future for technicians looks excellent. The U.S. Department of Labor estimates technician careers to grow at a rate of 22.2 percent through 2008. The overall growth rate for all jobs combined is estimated at 14.4 percent. As one writer put it, "As the farm hand was to the agrarian economy of a century ago and the machine operator was to the electromechanical industrial era of recent decades, the technician is becoming the core employee of the digital Information Age" (Louis S. Richman, "The New Worker Elite," *Fortune* 130 (1994): 56).

Technician careers are appealing for another, very practical reason: they are a short track to a good job. Most technician careers initially require two years or less of postsecondary training. A few require a bachelor's degree to be competitive, and a very few do not require a high school diploma. For the aspiring engineer more interested in the day to day, practical applications of engineering rather than the theoretical side of science, a career as an engineering technician may be perfect. Technicians often work right alongside the professionals. They are there for and often directly involved in the ground-breaking discoveries, long-awaited advances, and cutting-edge leaps. For a comparatively small investment in time and money, a person can emerge with a practical, highly marketable career.

Each article in this book discusses a particular technician occupation in detail, excluding medical technicians. (For information on medical technicians, see the companion book in this series, *Careers in Focus: Medical Technicians,* Second Edition. Ferguson Publishing, Chicago:1999.) The information comes from Ferguson's *Encyclopedia of Careers and Vocational Guidance.* The **History** section describes the history of the particular job as it relates to the overall development of its industry or field. The **Job** describes the primary and secondary duties of the job. **Requirements** discusses high school and postsecondary education and training requirements, any certification or licensing necessary, and any other personal requirements for success in the job. **Exploring** offers suggestions on how to gain some experience in or knowledge of the particular job before making a firm educational and financial commitment. The focus is on what can be done while still in high school (or in the early years of college) to gain a better understanding of the job. The **Employers** section gives an overview of typical places of employment for the job. **Starting Out** discusses the best ways to land that first job, be it through the college placement office, newspaper ads, or personal contact. The **Advancement** section describes what kind of career path to expect from the job and how to get there. **Earnings** lists salary ranges and describes the typical fringe benefits. The **Work Environment** section describes the typical surroundings and conditions of employment—whether indoors or outdoors, noisy or quiet, social or independent, and so on. Also discussed are typical hours worked, any seasonal fluctuations, and the stresses and strains of the job. The **Outlook** section summarizes the job in terms of the general economy and industry projections. For the most part, Outlook information is obtained from the Bureau of Labor Statistics and is supplemented by information taken from professional associations. Job growth terms follow those used in the *Occupational Outlook Handbook*: Growth described as "much faster than the average" means an increase of 36 percent or more. Growth described as "faster than the average" means an increase of 21 to 35 percent. Growth described as "about as fast as the average" means an increase of 10 to 20 percent. Growth described as "little change or more slowly than the average" means an increase of 0 to 9 percent. "Decline" means a decrease of 1 percent or more.

Each article ends with **For More Information**, which lists organizations that can provide career information on training, education, internships, scholarships, and job placement.

Agricultural Equipment Technicians

Overview

Agricultural equipment technicians work with modern farm machinery. They assemble, adjust, operate, maintain, modify, test, and even help design it. This machinery includes automatic animal feeding systems; milking machine systems; and tilling, planting, harvesting, irrigating, drying, and handling equipment. They work on farms or for agricultural machinery manufacturers or dealerships. They often supervise skilled mechanics and other workers who keep machines and systems operating at maximum efficiency.

History

The history of farming equipment stretches back to prehistoric times when the first agricultural workers developed the sickle. In the Middle Ages, the horse-drawn plow greatly increased farm production, and in the early 1700s,

Jethro Tull designed and built the first mechanical seed planter, further increasing production. The Industrial Revolution brought advances in the design and use of specialized machinery for strenuous and repetitive work. It had a great impact on the agricultural industry, beginning in 1831 with Cyrus McCormick's invention of the reaper.

In the first half of the 20th century governmental experiment stations developed high-yielding, standardized varieties of farm crops. This, combined with the establishment of agricultural equipment-producing companies, caused a boom in the production of farm machinery. In the late 1930s, the abundance of inexpensive petroleum spurred the development of gasoline- and diesel-run farm machinery. During the early 1940s, the resulting explosion in complex and powerful farm machinery multiplied production and replaced most of the horses and mules used on farms in the United States.

Modern farming is heavily dependent on very complex and expensive machinery. Highly trained and skilled technicians and farm mechanics are therefore required to install, operate, maintain, and modify it, thereby ensuring the nation's farm productivity. Recent developments in agricultural mechanization and automation make the career of agricultural equipment technicians both challenging and rewarding. Sophisticated machines are being used to plant, cultivate, harvest, and process food; to contour, drain, and renovate land; and to clear land and harvest forest products in the process. Qualified agricultural equipment technicians are needed not only to service and sell this equipment, but also to manage it on the farm.

Farming has increasingly become a highly competitive, big business. A successful farmer may have hundreds of thousands or even millions of dollars invested in land and machinery. For this investment to pay off, it is vital to keep the machinery in excellent operating condition. Prompt and reliable service from the farm equipment manufacturer and dealer is necessary for the success of both farmer and dealer. Interruptions or delays because of poor service are costly for everyone involved. To provide good service, manufacturers and dealers need technicians and specialists who possess agricultural and engineering knowledge in addition to technical skills.

The Job

Agricultural equipment technicians work in a wide variety of jobs both on and off the farm. In general, most agricultural equipment technicians find employment in one of three areas: equipment manufacturing, equipment sales and service, and on-farm equipment management.

Equipment manufacturing technicians are involved primarily with the design and testing of agricultural equipment such as farm machinery; irrigation, power, and electrification systems; soil and water conservation equipment; and agricultural harvesting and processing equipment. There are two kinds of technicians working in this field: agricultural engineering technicians and agricultural equipment test technicians.

Agricultural engineering technicians work under the supervision of design engineers. They prepare original layouts and complete detailed drawings of agricultural equipment. They also review plans, diagrams, and blueprints to ensure that new products comply with company standards and design specification. In order to do this they must use their knowledge of biological, engineering, and design principles. They also must keep current on all of the new equipment and materials being developed for the industry to make sure the machines run at their highest capacity.

Agricultural equipment test technicians test and evaluate the performance of agricultural machinery and equipment. In particular, they make sure the equipment conforms with operating requirements, such as horsepower, resistance to vibration, and strength and hardness of parts. They test equipment under actual field conditions on company-operated research farms and under more controlled conditions. They work with test equipment and recording instruments such as bend-fatigue machines, dynamometers, strength testers, hardness meters, analytical balances, and electronic recorders.

Test technicians are also trained in methods of recording the data gathered during these tests. They compute values such as horsepower and tensile strength using algebraic formulas and report their findings using graphs, tables, and sketches.

After the design and testing phases are complete, other agricultural equipment technicians work with engineers to perform any necessary adjustments in the equipment design. By performing these functions under the general supervision of the design engineer, technicians do the engineers' "detective work" so the engineers can devote more time to research and development.

Large agricultural machinery companies may employ agricultural equipment technicians to supervise production, assembly, and plant operations.

Most manufacturers market their products through regional sales organizations to individual dealers. Technicians may serve as sales representatives of regional sales offices, where they are assigned a number of dealers in a given territory and sell agricultural equipment directly to them. They may also conduct sales-training programs for the dealers to help them become more effective salespeople.

These technicians are also qualified to work in sales positions within dealerships, either as equipment sales workers or parts clerks. They are required to perform equipment demonstrations for customers. They also appraise the value of used equipment for trade-in allowances. Technicians in these positions may advance to sales or parts manager positions.

Some technicians involved in sales become systems specialists, who work for equipment dealerships, assisting farmers in the planning and installation of various kinds of mechanized systems, such as irrigation or materials-handling systems, grain bins, or drying systems.

In the service area, technicians may work as field service representatives, forming a liaison between the companies they represent and the dealers. They assist the dealers in product warranty work, diagnose service problems, and give seminars or workshops on new service information and techniques. These types of service technicians may begin their careers as specialists in certain kinds of repairs. Hydraulic specialists, for instance, maintain and repair the component parts of hydraulic systems in tractors and other agricultural machines. Diesel specialists rebuild, calibrate, and test diesel pumps, injectors, and other diesel engine components.

Many service technicians work as service managers or parts department managers. Service managers assign duties to the repair workers, diagnose machinery problems, estimate repair costs for customers, and manage the repair shop.

Parts department managers in equipment dealerships maintain inventories of all the parts that may be requested either by customers or by the service departments of the dealership. They deal directly with customers, parts suppliers, and dealership managers and must have good sales and purchasing skills. They also must be effective business managers.

Technicians working on the farm have various responsibilities, the most important of which is keeping machinery in top working condition during the growing season. During off-season periods they may overhaul or modify equipment or simply keep the machinery in good working order for the next season.

Some technicians find employment as on-farm machinery managers, usually working on large farms servicing or supervising the servicing of all automated equipment. They also monitor the field operation of all machines and keep complete records of costs, utilization, and repair procedures relating to the maintenance of each piece of mechanical equipment.

Requirements

High School

You should take as many mathematics courses as you can. You should also take technical/shop and mechanical drawing classes. Take science classes, including courses in earth science, to gain some insight into agriculture, soil conservation, and the environment. Look into adult education programs available to high school students; in such a program, you may be able to enroll in pre-engineering courses.

Postsecondary Training

A high school diploma is necessary, and some college and specialized experience is also important. A four-year education, along with some continuing education courses, can be very helpful in pursuing work, particularly if you're seeking jobs with the government.

Postsecondary education for the agricultural equipment technician should include courses in general agriculture, agricultural power and equipment, practical engineering, hydraulics, agricultural-equipment business methods, electrical equipment, engineering, social science, economics, and sales techniques. On-the-job experience during the summer is invaluable and frequently is included as part of the regular curriculum in these programs. Students are placed on farms, functioning as technicians-in-training. They also may work in farm equipment dealerships where their time is divided between the sales, parts, and service departments. Occupational experience, one of the most important phases of the postsecondary training program, gives students an opportunity to discover which field best suits them and which phase of the business they prefer. Upon completion of this program, most technical and community colleges award an associate's degree.

Other Requirements

The work of the agricultural equipment technician is similar to that of an engineer. You must have a knowledge of physical science and engineering principles and enough mathematical background to work with these principles. You must have a working knowledge of farm crops, machinery, and all agricultural-related products. You should be detail-oriented. You should also have people skills, as you'll be working closely with professionals, other technicians, and farmers.

Exploring

If you live in a farming community, you've probably already had some experience with farming equipment. Vocational agriculture education programs in high schools can be found in most rural settings, many suburban settings, and even in some urban schools. The teaching staff and counselors in these schools can provide considerable information about this career.

Light industrial machinery is now used in almost every industry. It is always helpful to watch machinery being used and to talk with people who own, operate, and repair it.

Summer and part-time work on a farm, in an agricultural equipment manufacturing plant, or in an equipment sales and service business offers opportunities to work on or near agricultural and light industrial machinery. Such a job may provide a clearer idea about the various activities, challenges, rewards, and possible limitations of this career.

Employers

Depending on your area of specialization, you'll be working for engineers, manufacturers, scientists, sales and services companies, and farmers. You can also find work with government agencies, such as the U.S. Department of Agriculture and the Agriculture Research Service.

Starting Out

It is still possible to enter this career by starting as an inexperienced worker in a machinery manufacturer's plant or on a farm and learning machine technician skills on the job. However, this approach is becoming increasingly difficult due to the complexity of modern machinery. Because of this, some formal classroom training is usually necessary, and many people find it difficult to complete even part-time study of the field's theory and science while also working a full-time job.

The demand for qualified agricultural equipment technicians currently exceeds the supply. Operators and managers of large, well-equipped farms and farm equipment companies in need of employees keep in touch with colleges offering agricultural equipment programs. Students who do well during their occupational experience period usually have an excellent chance of going to work for the same employer after graduation. Many colleges have an interview day on which personnel representatives of manufacturers, distributors, farm owners or managers, and dealers are invited to recruit students completing technician programs. In general, any student who does well in a training program can expect employment immediately upon graduation.

Advancement

Opportunities for advancement and self-employment are excellent for those with the initiative to keep abreast of continuing developments in the farm equipment field. Technicians often attend company schools in sales and service or take advanced evening courses in colleges.

Earnings

Agricultural technicians working for the government may be able to enter a position at GS-5 (government wage scale), which is around $23,000. Those with more education and specialized experience may be able to enter at GS-8, around $30,000. The 1998 Bureau of Labor Statistics tables list the weekly median wage of engineering and related technologists and technicians as $616. Those working on farms often receive room and board as a supplement to their annual salary. The salary that technicians eventually receive depends—as do most salaries—on individual ability, initiative, and the supply of skilled technicians in the field of work or locality. There is opportunity to work overtime during planting and harvesting seasons.

In addition to their salaries, most technicians receive fringe benefits such as health and retirement packages, paid vacations, and other benefits similar to those received by engineering technicians. Technicians employed in sales are usually paid a commission in addition to their base salary.

Work Environment

Working conditions vary according to the type of field chosen. The technician who is a part of a large farming operation will work indoors or outdoors depending on the season and the tasks that need to be done. Planning machine overhauls and the directing of such work usually are done in enclosed spaces equipped for it. As implied by its name, field servicing and repairs are done in the field.

Some agricultural equipment sales representatives work in their own or nearby communities, while others must travel extensively.

Technicians in agricultural equipment research, development, and production usually work under typical factory conditions: some work in an office or laboratory; others in a manufacturing plant; or, in some cases, field testing and demonstration are performed where the machinery will be used.

For technicians who assemble, adjust, modify, or test equipment and for those who provide customer service, application studies, and maintenance services, the surroundings may be similar to large automobile service centers.

In all cases, safety precautions must be a constant concern. Appropriate clothing, an acute awareness of one's environment, and careful lifting or hoisting of heavy machinery must be standard. While safety practices have improved greatly over the years, certain risks do exist. Heavy lifting may cause injury, and burns and cuts are always possible. The surroundings may be noisy and grimy. Some work is performed in cramped or awkward physical positions. Gasoline fumes and odors from oil products are a constant factor. Most technicians ordinarily work a 40-hour week, but emergency repairs may require overtime.

Outlook

The *Occupational Outlook Handbook* reports that employment of farm equipment mechanics is expected to decline. However, agricultural equipment businesses now demand more expertise than ever before. A variety of complex specialized machines and mechanical devices are steadily being produced and modified to help farmers improve the quality and productivity of their labor. These machines require trained technicians to design, produce, test, sell, and service them. Trained workers also are needed to instruct the final owners in their proper repair, operation, and maintenance.

In addition, the agricultural industry is adopting advanced computer and electronic technology. Computer skills are becoming more and more useful in this field. Precision farming will also require specialized training as agricultural equipment becomes hooked up to satellite systems.

As agriculture becomes more technical, the agricultural equipment technician will assume an increasingly vital role in helping farmers solve problems that interfere with efficient production. These opportunities exist not only in the United States, but also worldwide. As agricultural economies everywhere become mechanized, inventive technicians with training in modern business principles will find expanding employment opportunities abroad.

For More Information

To read equipment sales statistics, agricultural reports, and other news of interest to agricultural equipment technicians, visit the EMI Web site.

Equipment Manufacturers Institute (EMI)
10 South Riverside Plaza
Chicago, IL 60606-3710
Tel: 312-321-1470
Web: http://www.emi.org

At the FEMA Web site, you can learn about their publications and read industry news.

Farm Equipment Manufacturers Association (FEMA)
1000 Executive Parkway, Suite 100
St. Louis, MO 63141
Tel: 314-878-2304
Web: http://www.farmequip.org

Avionics Engineers and Technicians

School Subjects
Mathematics
Technical/Shop

Personal Skills
Mechanical/manipulative
Technical/scientific

Work Environment
Primarily indoors
Primarily one location

Minimum Education Level
Some postsecondary training

Salary Range
Engineers: $43,000 to $67,000 to $94,000+
Technicians: $20,000 to $38,000 to $50,000

Certification or Licensing
Required by all states

Outlook
More slowly than the average (engineers)
About as fast as the average (technicians)

Overview

Avionics (from the words aviation and electronics) is the application of electronics to the operation of aircraft, spacecraft, and missiles. *Avionics engineers* conduct research and solve developmental problems associated with aviation, such as instrument landing systems and other safety instruments. Avionics engineers held about 53,000 jobs in 1998. *Avionics technicians* inspect, test, adjust, and repair the electronic components of aircraft communications, navigation, and flight-control systems and compile complete maintenance-and-overhaul records for the work they do. Avionics technicians also calibrate and adjust the frequencies of communications apparatus when it is installed and perform periodic checks on those frequency settings. Avionics technicians held about 133,000 jobs in 1998.

History

The field of avionics grew out of World War II, when military aircraft were operated for the first time using electronic equipment. Rockets were also being developed during this time, and these devices required electronic systems to control their flight. As aircraft rapidly grew more complicated, the amount of electronic apparatus needed for navigation and for monitoring equipment performance greatly increased. The World War II B-29 bomber carried 2,000 to 3,000 avionic components; the B-52 of the Vietnam era carried 50,000; later, the B-58 supersonic bomber required more than 95,000. As the military grew increasingly reliant on electronic systems, specialists were required to build, install, operate, and repair them.

The development of large ballistic missiles during and after World War II and the rapid growth of the U.S. space program after 1958 increased development of avionics technology. Large missiles and spacecraft require many more electronic components than even the largest and most sophisticated aircraft. Computerized guidance systems became especially important with the advent of manned spaceflights. Avionics technology was also applied to civil aircraft. The race to be the first in space, and later, to be the first to land on the moon, stimulated the need for more and more trained specialists to work with newer and more complex electronic technology. The push for achieving military superiority during the Cold War era also created a demand for avionics specialists and technicians. From the 1950s to the present, the commercial airline industry grew rapidly; more and more planes were being built, and the drive to provide greater comfort and safety for passengers created still greater demand for avionics engineers and technicians.

Avionics continues to be an important branch of aeronautical and astronautical engineering. The aerospace industry places great emphasis on research and development, assigning a much higher percentage of its trained technical personnel to this effort than is usual in industry. In addition, stringent safety regulations require constant surveillance of in-service equipment. For these reasons there is a high demand for trained and experienced avionics engineers and technicians to help in the development of new satellites, spacecraft, aircraft, and their component electronic systems and to maintain those in service.

The Job

Avionics engineers develop new electronic systems and components for aerospace use. Avionics technicians assist engineers in these developments. They also adapt existing systems and components for application in new equipment. For the most part, however, they install, test, repair, and maintain navigation, communications, and control apparatus in existing aircraft and spacecraft.

Technicians use apparatus such as circuit analyzers and oscilloscopes to test and replace such sophisticated equipment as transceivers and Doppler radar systems, as well as microphones, headsets, and other standard electronic communications apparatus. New equipment, once installed, must be tested and calibrated to prescribed specifications. Technicians also adjust the frequencies of radio sets and other communications equipment by signaling ground stations and then adjusting set screws until the desired frequency has been achieved. Periodic maintenance checks and readjustments enable avionics technicians to keep equipment operating on proper frequencies. The technicians also complete and sign maintenance-and-overhaul documents recording the history of various equipment.

Avionics engineers and technicians involved in the design and testing of a new apparatus must take into account all operating conditions, determining weight limitations, resistance to physical shock, the atmospheric conditions the device will have to withstand, and other factors. For some sophisticated projects, technicians will have to design and make their tools first and then use them to construct and test new avionic components.

The range of equipment in the avionics field is so broad that technicians usually specialize in one area, such as radio equipment, radar, computerized guidance, or flight-control systems. New specialty areas are constantly opening up as innovations occur in avionics. The development of these new specialty areas requires technicians to keep informed by reading technical articles and books and by attending seminars and courses about the new developments, which are often sponsored by manufacturers.

Avionics technicians usually work as part of a team, especially if involved in research, testing, and development of new products. They are often required to keep notes and records of their work and to write detailed reports.

Requirements

High School

Persons interested in pursuing a career in avionics should take high school mathematics courses at least through solid geometry and preferably through calculus. They should take English, speech, and communications classes in order to read complex and detailed technical articles, books, and reports; to write technical reports; and to present those reports to groups of people when required. Many schools offer shop classes in electronics and in diagram and blueprint reading.

Postsecondary Training

Avionics engineers must have a bachelor's degree from an accredited college or university and may participate in a cooperative education program through their engineering school. Avionics technicians must have completed a course of training at a postsecondary technical institute or community college. The training should include at least one year of electronics technician training. If not trained specifically in avionics, students should obtain a solid background in electronics theory and practice. Further specialized training will be done on the job, where technicians work with engineers and senior technicians until they are competent to work without direct supervision.

Larger corporations in the aerospace industry operate their own schools and training institutes. Such training rarely includes theoretical or general studies but concentrates on areas important to the company's functions. The U.S. armed forces also conduct excellent electronics and avionics training schools; their graduates are in high demand in the industry after they leave the service.

Certification or Licensing

Federal Communications Commission (FCC) regulations require that anyone who works with radio transmitting equipment have a restricted radiotelephone operator's license. Such a license is issued upon application to the FCC and is issued for life.

Other Requirements

Students who are thinking about this kind of work should have strong science and mathematics skills. In addition, they will need to have good manual dexterity and mechanical aptitude and the temperament for exacting work.

Exploring

Students interested in avionics should visit factories and test facilities where avionics technicians work as part of teams designing and testing new equipment. It is also possible to visit a large airfield's repair facilities where avionics technicians inspect, maintain, and calibrate communications and control apparatus. Students can also arrange to visit other types of electronics manufacturers.

Useful information about avionics training programs and career opportunities is available from the U.S. armed forces as well as from trade and technical schools and community colleges that offer such programs. These organizations are always pleased to answer inquiries from prospective students or service personnel.

Employers

Aerospace corporations are the primary employers of avionics technicians and engineers. Some may work in repair and maintenance at large airfields. Avionics training and employment is also available in the military.

Starting Out

Those entering the field of avionics must first obtain the necessary training in electronics. Following that training, the school's placement officer can help locate prospective employers, arrange interviews, and advise about an employment search. Other possibilities are to contact an employment agency or to approach a prospective employer directly. Service in the military is an excellent way to gain education, training, and experience in avionics; many companies are eager to hire technicians with a military background.

Advancement

Avionics technicians usually begin their careers in trainee positions until they are thoroughly familiar with the requirements and routines of their work. Having completed their apprenticeships, they are usually assigned to work independently, with only minimal supervision, doing testing and repair work. The most experienced and able technicians go on to install new equipment and to work in research and development operations. Many senior technicians move into training, supervisory, sales, and customer relations positions. Some choose to pursue additional training and become avionics engineers.

Avionics engineers are already at an advanced position but may move up to become engineering supervisors or managers.

Earnings

Avionics engineers earn from $43,000 to $67,000 to more than $94,000 a year. Median earnings of avionics technicians were about $38,000 in 1998. Beginning avionics technicians earn about $18,000 to $20,000 a year. The top 10 percent of technicians earns more than $50,000 a year. The lowest ten percent earned less than $25,000 a year. Federal government employees (not including armed forces personnel) on the average earn slightly less than avionics technicians employed by private aerospace firms. Their jobs, on the other hand, have greater security.

Work Environment

Avionics engineers and technicians work for aircraft and aerospace manufacturers, airlines, and NASA and other government agencies. Most avionics engineers and technicians specialize in a specific area of avionics; they are also responsible for keeping up with the latest technological and industry advances. Their work is usually performed in pleasant indoor surroundings. Because this work is very precise, successful engineers and technicians must have a personality suited to meeting exact standards and working within small tolerances. Technicians sometimes work in closely cooperating teams. This requires an ability to work with a team spirit of coordinated effort.

Outlook

The aerospace industry is closely tied to government spending and to political change, as well as to the economy, which also affects the aircraft and airline industries strongly. The cancellation of one spacecraft program or a fall in airline travel that leads to employee cutbacks may throw a large number of avionics technicians out of work, making competition for the remaining jobs very keen. The defense industry has suffered severe declines since the end of the Cold War and the resulting decreases in military spending. Since 1989, the aerospace industry has cut nearly 500,000 jobs. In 1994 alone, nearly 80,000 jobs were lost across the aerospace industry.

On the positive side, avionics is an important and constantly developing field for which more and more trained technicians will be required. Reliance on electronic technology has grown rapidly and in virtually every industry. Many defense contractors have begun to branch out into other products, especially in the areas of electronic and computer technology. Commercial applications of the space program, including the launching of privately owned satellites, are providing new opportunities in the aerospace industry.

Employment for avionics engineers is expected to grow more slowly than the average. Employment for avionics technicians is expected to increase about as fast as the average through 2008. Population growth and higher incomes are expected to bring about an increase in the demand for airline transportation. And while the number of aircraft is expected to grow, the number of jobs available will be affected by the increase in automated systems.

For More Information

Contact the following organization for information on avionics careers:

General Aviation Manufacturers Association
1400 K Street, NW, Suite 801
Washington, DC 20005
Tel: 202-393-1500
Web: http://www.generalaviation.org/

For information on careers, lists of schools, and scholarships, contact:

National Air Transportation Association
4226 King Street
Alexandria, VA 22302
Tel: 703-845-9000
Web: http://www.nata-online.org

Aerospace Industries Association of America
1250 Eye Street, NW, Suite 1200
Washington, DC 20005-3922
Tel: 202-371-8400
Web: http://www.aia-aerospace.org/

For career information, see AIAC's Web site:

Aerospace Industries Association of Canada (AIAC)
60 Queen Street, #1200
Ottawa, ON K1P 5Y7 Canada
Tel: 613-232-4297
Web: http://www.aiac.ca

Chemical Technicians

Chemistry Mathematics	School Subjects
Following instructions Technical/scientific	Personal Skills
Primarily indoors Primarily one location	Work Environment
Some postsecondary training	Minimum Education Level
$21,000 to $31,000 to $42,000	Salary Range
None available	Certification or Licensing
More slowly than the average	Outlook

Overview

Chemical technicians assist chemists and chemical engineers in the research, development, testing, and manufacturing of chemicals and chemical-based products.

History

Modern chemistry goes back thousands of years to the earliest days when humans extracted medicinal juices from plants and shaped metals into tools and utensils for daily life. In the late 18th century, chemistry became established as a science when Antoine Lavoisier formulated the law of the conservation of matter. From that time until the present, the number and types of products attributed to the development and expansion of chemistry is almost incalculable.

The period following World War I witnessed an enormous expansion of chemical technology and its application to the production of goods and consumer products such as high octane gasoline, antifreeze, pesticides, pharmaceuticals, plastics, and artificial fibers and fabrics. This rapid expansion increased the need for professionally trained chemists and technicians. The technicians, with their basic chemical knowledge and manual skills, were able to handle the tasks that did not require the specialized education of their bosses. These nonprofessionals sometimes had the title of *junior chemist.*

During the last 30 years, however, there has been a radical change in the status of the chemical technician from a "mere" assistant to a core professional. Automation and computerization have increased laboratory efficiency and corporate downsizing has eliminated many layers of intermediate hierarchy. The result has been to increase the level of responsibility and independence, meaning greater recognition of the importance of today's highly skilled and trained chemical technicians.

The Job

Most chemical technicians who work in the chemical industry are involved in the development, testing, and manufacturing of plastics, paints, detergents, synthetic fibers, industrial chemicals, and pharmaceuticals. Others work in the petroleum, aerospace, metals, electronics, automotive, and construction industries. Some chemical technicians work in universities and government laboratories.

They may work in any of the fields of chemistry, such as analytical, biochemistry, inorganic, organic, physical, or any of the many subbranches of chemistry. Chemical engineering, which is a combination of chemistry and engineering, develops or improves manufacturing processes for making commercial amounts of chemicals, many of which were previously produced only in small quantities in laboratory glassware or a pilot plant.

Within these subfields, chemical technicians work in research and development, design and production, and quality control. In research and development, chemical laboratory technicians often work with Ph.D. chemists and chemical engineers to set up and monitor laboratory equipment and instruments, prepare laboratory setups, and record data.

Technicians often determine the chemical composition, concentration, stability, and level of purity on a wide range of materials. These may include ores, minerals, pollutants, foods, drugs, plastics, dyes, paints, detergents, chemicals, paper, and petroleum products. Although chemists or chemical engineers may design an experiment, technicians help them create process designs, develop written procedures, or devise computer simulations. They also select all necessary glassware, reagents, chemicals, and equipment. Technicians also perform analyses and report test results.

In the design and production area, chemical technicians work closely with chemical engineers to monitor the large-scale production of compounds and to help develop and improve the processes and equipment used. They prepare tables, charts, sketches, diagrams, and flow charts that record and summarize the collected data.

They work with pipelines, valves, pumps, and metal and glass tanks. Chemical technicians often use their input to answer manufacturing questions, such as how to transfer materials from one point to another, and to build, install, modify, and maintain processing equipment. They also train and supervise production operators. They may operate small-scale equipment for determining process parameters.

Fuel technicians determine viscosities of oils and fuels, measure flash points (the temperature at which fuels catch fire), pour points (the coldest temperature at which the fuel can flow), and the heat output of fuels.

Pilot plant operators make erosion and corrosion tests on new construction materials to determine their suitability. They prepare chemicals for field testing and report on the effectiveness of new design concepts.

Applied research technicians help design new manufacturing or research equipment.

Requirements

High School

Several years of science and mathematics should be taken in high school, and computer training is also important. While a minority of employers still hire high school graduates and place them into their own training programs, the majority prefer to hire graduates of community colleges who have completed two-year chemical technician programs or even bachelor degree recipients. If a four-year college enrollment is planned, as much as three years of high school mathematics, including algebra, geometry, and trigonometry; three years of physical sciences, including chemistry; and four years of English should be studied.

Postsecondary Training

Graduates of community college programs are productive much sooner than untrained individuals because they have the technical knowledge and laboratory experience and skills for the job. Computer courses are necessary as computers and computer-interfaced equipment are routinely used in the field. Realizing that many students become aware of technical career possibilities too late to satisfy college requirements, many community and technical colleges that offer chemical technician programs may also have noncredit courses that allow students to meet college entrance requirements.

About 40 two-year colleges in the United States have chemical technology programs. Once enrolled in a two-year college program designed for chemical technicians, students should expect to take a number of chemistry courses with strong emphasis on laboratory work and the presentation of data. These courses will include basic concepts of modern chemistry, such as atomic structure, descriptive chemistry of both organic and inorganic substances, analytical methods including quantitative and instrumental analysis, and physical properties of substances. Other courses include communications, physics, mathematics, industrial safety, and organic laboratory equipment and procedures.

Other Requirements

Besides the educational requirements, certain personal characteristics are necessary for successful chemical technicians. They must have both the ability and the desire to use mental and manual skills. They should also have a good supply of patience because experiments must frequently be repeated several times. They should be precise and like doing detailed work. Mechanical aptitude and good powers of observation are also needed. They should be able to follow directions closely and enjoy solving problems. Chemical technicians also need excellent organizational and communication skills. Other important qualities are a desire to learn new skills and a willingness to accept responsibility. In addition, technicians should have good eyesight, color perception, and eye-hand coordination.

Exploring

Students should join their high school science clubs or organizations, as well as take part in extracurricular activities such as the Junior Engineering Technical Society (JETS). Science contests are a good way to apply principles learned in classes to a special project. Students can also subscribe to the American Chemical Society's *Chem Matters*, a quarterly magazine for students taking chemistry in high school. Examples of topics covered in the magazine include the chemistry of lipstick, suntan products, contact lenses, and carbon-14 dating. Also, qualifying students can participate in Project SEED (Summer Education Experience for the Disadvantaged), a summer program designed to provide high school students from economically disadvantaged homes with the opportunity to experience science research in a laboratory environment.

College students can become student affiliates of professional associations such as the American Chemical Society and the American Institute of Chemical Engineers. Membership allows students to experience the professionalism of a career in chemistry. They can also contact ACS or AIChE local sections to talk with chemists and chemical engineers about what they do. These associations can also help them find summer or co-op work experiences. All these opportunities can help determine if a career in chemistry is a good choice.

Employers

Almost all chemical laboratories, no matter their size or function, employ chemical technicians to assist their chemists or chemical engineers with research as well as routine laboratory work. Therefore, chemical technicians can find employment wherever chemistry is involved: in industrial laboratories, government agencies such as the Departments of Health or Agriculture, or at colleges and universities. They can work in almost any field of chemical activity, such as industrial manufacturing of all kinds, pharmaceuticals, food, and production of chemicals.

Starting Out

Graduates of chemical technology programs often find jobs during the last term of their two-year programs. Some companies work with local community colleges and technical schools to maintain a supply of trained chemical technicians. Recruiters regularly visit most colleges where chemical technology programs are offered. Most employers recruit locally or regionally. Because companies hire locally and work closely with technical schools, placement offices are usually successful in finding jobs for their graduates.

Some recruiters also go to four-year colleges and look for chemists with bachelor's degrees. Whether a company hires bachelor's-level chemists or two-year chemical technology graduates depends upon both the outlook of the company and the local supply of graduates.

Internships and co-op work are highly regarded by employers, and participation in such programs is a good way to get a foot in the door. Many two- and four-year schools have co-op programs in which full-time students work about 20 hours a week for a local company. Such programs may be available to high school seniors as well. Students in these programs develop a good knowledge of the employment possibilities and frequently stay with their co-op employers.

More and more companies are using contract workers to perform technicians' jobs, and this is another way to enter the field. There are local agencies that place technicians with companies for special projects or temporary assignments that last anywhere from a month to a year or more. Many of these contract workers are later hired on a full-time basis.

Advancement

Competent chemical technicians can expect to have long-term career paths. Top research and development positions are open to technically trained people, whether they start out with an associate's degree in chemical technology, a bachelor's degree in chemistry, or just a lot of valuable experience with no degree. There are also opportunities for advancement in the areas of technology development or technology management, providing comparable pay for these separate but equal paths. Some companies have the same career path for all technicians, regardless of education level. Other companies have different career ladders for technicians and chemists but will promote qualified technicians to chemists and move them up that path. Advancement opportunities at Fortune 500 companies are particularly plentiful.

Some companies may require additional formal schooling for promotion, and the associate's degree can be a stepping stone toward a bachelor's degree in chemistry. Many companies encourage their technicians to continue their education, and most reimburse tuition costs. Continuing education in the form of seminars, workshops, and in-company presentations is also important for advancement. Chemical technicians who want to advance must keep up with current developments in the field by reading trade and technical journals and publications.

Earnings

The median salary in 1998 for all science technicians and technologists was $31,000 according to the Bureau of Labor Statistics. Ten percent earned less than $21,000 and 10 percent earned over $42,000. The median earnings for chemical technicians working in research and testing were $24,000. Those who worked in drug manufacturing earned $32,000. Salaries are highest in private industry and lowest in colleges and universities. Salaries vary by the education, experience, and responsibility level of technicians as well as the type and size of the company where they are employed. The greatest variation in salary is from region to region. Starting salaries are highest in the Middle Atlantic region and lowest in the East South Central region. If technicians belong to a union, wages and benefits depend on the union agreement. However, the percentage of technicians who belong to a union is very small. Benefits depend on the employer, but they usually include paid vacations and holidays, insurance, and tuition refund plans. Technicians normally work a five-day, 40-hour week. Occasional overtime may be necessary.

Work Environment

The chemical industry is one of the safest industries in which to work. Laboratories and plants normally have safety committees and safety engineers who closely monitor equipment and practices to minimize hazards. Chemical technicians usually receive safety training both in school and at work to recognize potential hazards and to take appropriate measures.

Most chemical laboratories are clean and well lighted. Chemical technicians usually have very few people working in the immediate area. Technicians often work at tables and benches while operating laboratory equipment and are usually provided office or desk space to record data or prepare reports. The work can sometimes be monotonous and repetitive, as when making samples or doing repetitive testing. Chemical plants are usually clean, and the number of operating personnel for the space involved is often very low.

Outlook

Employment of science technicians will increase more slowly than the average through 2008, according to the *Occupational Outlook Handbook*. Employment prospects are better in specialty chemicals and parts of the industry that sell directly to consumers, such as pharmaceutical firms. Technologies expected to grow include biotechnology, environment, catalysis, materials science, communication and computer technology, and energy. Business areas with the most potential for growth include environmental services and "earth-friendly" products, analytical development and services, custom or niche products and services, and quality control. Growth, however, will be offset by a general slowdown in overall employment in the chemical industry.

Graduates of chemical technology programs will continue to face competition from bachelor's level chemists. The chemical and chemical-related industries will continue to become increasingly sophisticated in both their products and their manufacturing techniques. Automation, new products, and complex production methods assure the demand for trained technicians.

For More Information

A list of chemical technology programs and single copies of other career materials are free. A directory of opportunities listing internships, summer jobs, and co-op programs is available for a fee. Contact:

American Chemical Society
Career Education
1155 16th Street, NW
Washington, DC 20036
Tel: 202-452-2113
Web: http://www.acs.org

Computer and Office Machine Service Technicians

School Subjects Computer science Technical/shop	
Personal Skills Mechanical/manipulative Technical/scientific	
Work Environment Primarily indoors Primarily multiple locations	
Minimum Education Level High school diploma	
Salary Range $16,000 to $30,000 to $48,000	
Certification or Licensing Recommended	
Outlook Faster than the average	

Overview

Computer and office machine service technicians install, calibrate, maintain, troubleshoot, and repair equipment such as computers and their peripherals, office equipment, and specialized electronic equipment used in many factories, hospitals, airplanes, and numerous other businesses. Potential employers include computer companies and large corporations that need a staff devoted to repair and maintain their equipment. Many service technicians are employed by companies that contract their services to other businesses. According to the *Occupational Outlook Handbook*, computer and office machine service technicians held about 138,000 jobs in 1998.

History

When computers were first introduced to the business world, businesses found their size to be cumbersome and their capabilities limited. Today, technological advances have made computers smaller, yet more powerful in their speed and capabilities. As more businesses rely on computers and other office machines to help manage daily activities, access information, and link offices and resources, the need for experienced professionals to work and service these machines will increase. Service technicians are employed by many corporations, hospitals, and the government, as part of a permanent staff, or may be contracted to work for other businesses.

The Job

L3 Communications manufactures computer systems for a diverse group of clients such as Shell Oil, United Airlines, and the Chicago Board of Trade. Besides computer systems, they also offer services such as equipment maintenance contracts and customer training. Joey Arca, a service technician for L3 Communications, loves the challenge and diversity of his job. He and other members of the staff are responsible for the installation of computer mainframes and systems, as well as training employees on the equipment. A large part of their work is the maintenance, diagnosis, and repair of computer equipment. Since the clients are located throughout the United States, Arca must often travel to different cities in his assigned district. He also presents company products and services to potential clients, and bids for maintenance contracts.

"I don't always have to be at the office—which gives me a lot of freedom," says Arca. "Sometimes I call in from my home and get my scheduled appointments for the day." The freedom of not being deskbound does have its downfalls. "One of the most difficult part of the job is not knowing when a computer will fail. I carry a pager 24/7, and if I get called, I'm bound to a two-hour response time."

Many times work is scheduled before or after regular working hours, or else on the weekend since it's important to have the least amount of workday disruption. Arca is successful in his job because he keeps on top of technology that is constantly changing by way of continuing education classes and training seminars. He is also well versed in both hardware and software, especially system software.

When asked what kind of people are best suited for this line of work, Arca replied, "task oriented, quantitatively smart, organized, and personable. Also, they need the ability to convey technical terms in writing and orally."

Requirements

High School

Traditional high school courses such as mathematics, physical sciences, and other laboratory-based sciences can provide a strong foundation for understanding basic mechanical and electronics principles. English and speech classes can help boost your written and verbal communications skills.

Postsecondary Training

A high school diploma is the minimum requirement for pursuing a career in this field, though many have advanced degrees. Arca, for example, holds a bachelor of science degree in electrical engineering. He credits specialized classes such as Voice and Data Communications, Microprocessor Controls, and Digital Circuits as giving him a good base for his current work environment.

Certification or Licensing

Certification is required by most employers though standards vary depending on the company. However, it is considered by many as a measure of industry knowledge. Certification can also give you a competitive edge when interviewing for a new job, or negotiating for a higher salary.

A variety of certification programs are available from the International Society of Certified Electronics Technicians, and the Institute for Certification of Computing Professionals, among other organizations. After the successful completion of study and examination, you may be certified in fields such as computer, industrial, and electronic equipment. Continuing education credits are required for recertification, usually every two to four years. Arca is certified as a computer technician from the Association of Energy Engineers, and the Electronics Technicians Association and Satellite Dealers Association.

Other Requirements

A strong technical background and an aptitude for learning about new technologies, good communications skills, and superior manual dexterity, will help you succeed in this industry. You'll also need to be motivated to keep up with modern computer and office machine technology. Machines rapidly become obsolete, and so does the service technician's training. When new equipment is installed, service technicians must demonstrate the intellectual agility to learn how to handle problems that might arise.

Employers

Though work opportunities for service technicians are available nationwide, many jobs are located in large cities where computer companies and larger corporations are based. Arca's employer, like many other service contractors, is headquartered in Anaheim, California, but maintains satellite offices throughout the United States.

Starting Out

If your school offers placement services, take them up on it. Many times, school placements and counseling centers are privy to job openings that are filled before being advertised in the newspaper. Make sure your counselors know of any important preferences—location, specialization, and other requirements—so they can best match you to an employer. Don't forget to supply them with an updated resume.

There are also other avenues to take when searching for a job in this industry. Many jobs are advertised in the Jobs section of your local newspaper. Look under "Computers" or "Electronics." Also, inquire directly with the personnel department of companies that appeal to you and fill out an application. Trade association Web sites are good sources of job leads; many will post employment opportunities as well as allow you to post your resume.

Advancement

Due to the growth of computer products and their influence over the business world, this industry offers a variety of advancement opportunities. Service technicians usually start by working on relatively simple maintenance and repair tasks. Over time, they start working on more complicated projects.

Experienced service technicians may advance to positions of increased responsibility, such as a crew supervisor or a departmental manager. Another advancement route is to become a sales representative for a computer manufacturing company. Technicians develop hands-on knowledge of particular machines and are thus often in the best position to advise potential buyers about important purchasing decisions. Some entrepreneurial-minded servicers might open their own repair business, which can be risky but can also provide many rewards. Unless they fill a certain market niche, technicians usually find it necessary to service a wide range of computers and office machines.

Earnings

According to the *Occupational Outlook Handbook*, in 1998, service technicians specializing in communications and industrial electronic equipment earned an average annual salary of $31,304; while computer equipment service technicians earned an average of $30,264 a year. Technicians with extensive work experience and certification earn more.

Standard work benefits include health and life insurance, paid vacation and sick time, as well as a retirement plan. Most technicians are given travel stipends; some receive company cars.

Work Environment

"I like the freedom of not working in a (typical) office environment and the short work weeks," says Arca. Most service technicians, however, have unpredictable work schedules. Some weeks are quiet and may warrant fewer work hours. However, during a major computer problem, or worse yet, a breakdown, technicians are required to work around the clock to fix the problem as quickly as possible. Technicians spend a considerable time on call, and must carry a pager in case of work emergencies.

Travel is an integral part of the job for many service technicians, many times amounting to 80 percent of the job time. Arca has even traveled to the Philippines where he worked on the Tomahawk Missile project at Clark Air Force Base. Since he is originally from the Philippines, he was able to combine work with a visit with friends and family.

Outlook

According to the *Occupational Outlook Handbook*, employment opportunities for service technicians working with computer and office equipment are expected to grow faster than the average—about 34 percent faster than the average for all other occupations. Demand for service technicians specializing in commercial and industrial electronic equipment is expected to grow about 12 percent. As corporations, the government, hospitals, and universities worldwide continue their reliance on computers to help manage their daily business, demand for qualified and skilled technicians will increase.

Modern office equipment is better designed and can run longer without needing maintenance or repair. As a result, demand for service technicians specializing in office equipment repair is expected to grow only as fast as the average.

For More Information

For certification information, contact:

Institute for Certification of Computing Professionals
2200 East Devon Avenue, Suite 247
Des Plaines, IL 60018-4503
Tel: 847-299-4227
Web: http://www.iccp.org

For industry information or details on their certification program, contact:

International Society of Certified Electronics Technicians
2708 West Berry Street
Fort Worth, TX 76109-2356
Tel: 817-921-9101
Web: http://www.iscet.org

Contact ACM for information on internships, student membership, and the ACM magazine, Crossroads. *ACM also has a student Web site at http://www.acm.org/membership/student/.*

Association for Computing Machinery (ACM)
1515 Broadway, 17th Floor
New York, NY 10036-5701
Tel: 212-869-7440
Email: SIGS@acm.org
Web: http://www.acm.org

For certification, career, and placement information, contact:

Electronics Technicians Association and Satellite Dealers Association
602 North Jackson
Greencastle, IN 46135
Tel: 765-653-4301
Web: http://www.eta-sda.com

Computer-Aided Design Drafters and Technicians

School Subjects	
Computer science	
Mathematics	
Technical/Shop	
Personal Skills	
Mechanical/manipulative	
Technical/scientific	
Work Environment	
Primarily indoors	
Primarily one location	
Minimum Education Level	
High school diploma	
Salary Range	
$17,000 to $32,000 to $52,000	
Certification or Licensing	
Voluntary	
Outlook	
More slowly than the average	

Overview

Computer-aided design drafters and technicians, sometimes called *CAD technicians* or *CAD designers*, use computer-based systems to produce or revise technical illustrations needed in the design and development of machines, products, buildings, manufacturing processes, and other work. They use CAD machinery to manipulate and create design concepts so that they are feasible to produce and use in the real world.

History

Just over 30 years ago, drafting and designing were done with a pencil and paper on a drafting board. To make a circle, drafters used a compass. To draw straight lines and the correct angles, they used a straight-edge, slide rule, and other tools. With every change required before a design was right, it was "back to the drawing board" to get out the eraser, sharpen the pencil, and revise the drawing. Everybody did it this way, whether the design was simple or complex: automobiles, hammers, printed circuit boards, utility piping, highways, or buildings.

CAD/CAM technology came about in the 1970s with the development of microprocessors (computer processors in the form of miniaturized integrated circuits contained on tiny silicon chips). Microprocessors opened up many new uses for computers by greatly reducing the size of computers while also increasing their power and speed.

Amazingly enough, the drafters and designers working to develop these microprocessors were also the first to benefit from this technology. As the circuits on the silicon chips that the designers were working on became too complex to diagram by pencil and paper, the designers began to use the chips themselves to help store information, create models, and produce diagrams for the design of new chip circuits. This was just the beginning of computer-assisted design and drafting technology. Today, there are tens of thousands of CAD workstations in industrial settings. The use of CAD systems greatly speed and simplify the designer's and drafter's work. They do more than just let the operator "draw" the technical illustration on the screen. They add the speed and power of computer processing, plus software with technical information that ease the designer/drafter's tasks. CAD systems make complex mathematical calculations, spot problems, offer advice, and provide a wide range of other assistance. Today, nearly all drafting tasks are done with such equipment.

As the Internet has developed along with the use of email, CAD operators can send a CAD drawing across the world in a matter of minutes attached to an email message. Gone are the days of rolling up a print and mailing it off. Technology has once again made work more efficient for the CAD designer and drafter.

The Job

Technicians specializing in CAD technology usually work in the design and drafting activities associated with new product research and development, although many work in other areas such as structural mechanics or piping. CAD technicians must combine drafting and computer skills. They work in any field where detailed drawings, diagrams, and layouts are important aspects of developing new product designs—for example, in architecture, electronics, and in the manufacturing of automobiles, aircraft, computers, and missiles and other defense systems. Most CAD technicians specialize in a particular industry or on one part of a design.

CAD technicians work under the direction and supervision of *CAD engineers and designers*, experts highly trained in applying computer technology to industrial design and manufacturing. These designers and engineers plan how to relate the CAD technology and equipment to the design process. They are also the ones who give assignments to the CAD technicians.

Jackie Sutherland started as a drafter right out of high school, working at a major Midwestern diesel engine manufacturer. Since then, he has moved into a designer's role. In his 25 years on the job, he has seen the transfer from drafting board to CAD workstation.

"I work with everyone from the customer to the engineers, suppliers, pattern makers, and the assembly line from the project concept through the production," says Sutherland of his work as a CAD designer.

Technicians work at specially designed and equipped interactive computer graphics workstations. They call up computer files that hold data about a new product; they then run the programs to convert that information into diagrams and drawings of the product. These are displayed on a video display screen, which then acts as an electronic drawing board. Following the directions of a CAD engineer or designer, the CAD technician enters changes to the product's design into the computer. The technician then merges these changes into the data file, then displays the corrected diagrams and drawings.

The software in CAD systems is very helpful to the user—it offers suggestions and advice and even points out errors. The most important advantage of working with a CAD system is that it saves the technician from the lengthy process of having to produce, by hand, the original and then the revised product drawings and diagrams.

The CAD workstation is equipped to allow technicians to perform calculations, develop simulations, and manipulate and modify the displayed material. Using typed commands at a keyboard, a stylus or light pen for touching the screen display, a mouse, joystick, or other electronic methods of interacting with the display, technicians can move, rotate, or zoom in on any aspect of the drawing on the screen, and project three-dimensional images from two-dimensional sketches. They can make experimental changes to the design and then run tests on the modified design to determine its qualities, such as weight, strength, flexibility, and the cost of materials that would be required. Compared to traditional drafting and design techniques, CAD offers virtually unlimited freedom to explore alternatives, and in far less time.

When the product design is completed and the necessary information is assembled in the computer files, technicians may store the newly developed data, output it on a printer, transfer it to another computer, or send it directly to another step of the automated testing or manufacturing process.

Once the design is approved for production, CAD technicians may use their computers to assist in making detailed drawings of certain parts of the design. They may also prepare designs and drawings of the tools or equipment, such as molds, cutting tools, and jigs, that must be specially made in order to manufacture the product. As the product moves toward production, technicians, drafters, and designers may work closely with those assembling the product to ensure the same quality found with prototype testing.

CAD technicians must keep records of all of their test procedures and results. They may need to present written reports, tables, or charts to document their test results or other findings. If a particular system, subsystem, or material has not met a testing or production requirement, technicians may be asked to suggest a way to rearrange the system's components or substitute alternate materials.

The company Sutherland works for also uses interoffice and Internet email to communicate with coworkers and the outside world. "I can attach text, a spreadsheet, or a complete three-dimensional CAD model to a message and send it out to several people through a distribution list. It really shortens the cycle of time on a project," he says.

Requirements

High School

CAD technicians must be able to read and understand complex engineering diagrams and drawings. The minimum educational requirement for CAD technicians is a high school diploma. If you are a high school student, take courses that provide you with a solid background in algebra, geometry, trigonometry, physics, machine-shop skills, drafting, and electronics, and take whatever computer courses are available. You should also take courses in English, especially those that improve your communication skills.

Postsecondary Training

Increasingly, most prospective CAD technicians are undertaking formal training beyond the high school level, usually in a two-year associate's degree program taught at a technical school or community college.

Such a program should include courses in these basic areas: basic drafting, machine drawing, architecture, civil drafting (with an emphasis on highways), process piping, electrical, electrical instrumentation, HVAC, and plumbing. There should also be courses in data processing; computer programming, systems, and equipment, especially video-display equipment; computer graphics; product design; and computer peripheral equipment and data storage. Some two-year programs may also require you to complete courses in technical writing, communications, social sciences, and the humanities.

In addition, some companies have their own training programs, which can last as long as two years. Requirements for entry into these company-run training programs vary from company to company.

If you are considering a career in CAD technology it is important to remember that you will be required to take continuing-education courses even after you have found a job. This continuing education is necessary because technicians need to know about recent advances in technology that may affect procedures, equipment, terminology, or programming concepts.

"Technology changes so fast in this area," says Sutherland of his many years in the drafting and designing field.

Certification or Licensing

Certification for CAD technicians is voluntary. Certification in drafting is available from the American Design and Drafting Association (ADDA), which invites members and nonmembers regardless of formal training or experience to participate in its Drafter Certification Program. The certification process includes taking a 90-minute test of basic drafting skills, but does not include testing of CAD drafting.

Licensing requirements vary. Licensing may be required for specific projects, such as a construction project, when the client requires it.

Other Requirements

As a CAD technician or designer, you will need to think logically, have good analytical skills, and be methodical, accurate, and detail-oriented in all your work. You should be able to work as part of a team, as well as independently, since you will spend long periods of time in front of video display screens.

"You have to be able to visualize what a part may look like or what a new version of a part may look like," says Sutherland. "You have to have basic common sense but also be able to look into the future."

Exploring

There are a number of ways to gain firsthand knowledge about the field of CAD technology. Unfortunately, part-time or summer jobs involved directly with CAD technology are very hard to find; however, drafting-related jobs can sometimes be found, and many future employers will look favorably on applicants with this kind of experience. In addition, jobs related to other engineering fields, such as electronics or mechanics, may be available, and can offer you an opportunity to become familiar with the kind of workplace in which technicians may later be employed.

In addition, high school courses in computers, geometry, physics, mechanical drawing, and shop work will give you a feel for the mental and physical activities associated with CAD technology. Other relevant activities include membership in high school science clubs (especially computer and electronics clubs); participating in science fairs; pursuing hobbies that involve computers, electronics, drafting, mechanical equipment, and model building; and reading books and articles about technical topics.

Employers

CAD drafters and technicians are employed in a wide variety of industries, including engineering, architecture, manufacturing, construction, communication, utilities, and the government. They are employed by both large and small companies throughout the United States. For some specialties, jobs may be more specific to certain locations. For example, a drafter or designer for the software industry will find the most opportunities in California's Silicon Valley, while an automotive specialist may be more successful finding jobs near Detroit, Michigan.

Starting Out

Probably the most reliable method for entering this field is through your school's placement office. This is especially true for students who graduate from a two-year college or technical institute: recruiters from companies employing CAD technicians sometimes visit such schools, and placement office personnel can help students meet with these recruiters.

As a graduate of a postsecondary program, you can conduct your own job search by contacting architects, building firms, manufacturers, high technology companies, and government agencies. You can contact prospective employers by phone or with a letter stating your interest in employment, accompanied by a resume that provides details about your education and job experience. State or private employment agencies may also be helpful, and classified ads in newspapers and professional journals may provide additional leads.

Advancement

CAD technicians who demonstrate their ability to handle more responsibility can expect to receive promotions after just a few years on the job. They may be assigned to designing work that requires their special skills or experience, such as troubleshooting problems with systems they have worked with; or they may be promoted to supervisory or training positions. As trainers, they may teach courses at their workplace or at a local school or community college.

In general, as CAD technicians advance, their assignments become less and less routine, until they may have a hand in designing and building equipment. Technicians who continue their education and earn a bachelor's degree may become data processing managers, engineers, or systems analysts or manufacturing analysts.

Other routes for advancement include becoming a sales representative for a design firm or for a company selling computer-assisted design services or equipment. It may also be possible to become an independent contractor for companies using or manufacturing CAD equipment.

Earnings

According to the American Design and Drafting Association (ADDA) 1996 salary survey, apprentice CAD drafters can expect to make an average of $17,316 per year. The most experienced CAD designers can expect an average of $49,504 per year, with a median salary of $33,410.

The *Occupational Outlook Handbook* reports that the median earnings of drafters in 1998 were $32,364. The lowest 10 percent earned less than 21,195 and the highest 10 percent earned more than $51,667.

Actual salaries will vary widely depending on geographic location, exact job requirements, and the training needed to obtain those jobs. With increased training and experience, technicians can earn higher salaries, and some technicians with special skills, extensive experience, or added responsibilities may earn more.

Benefits usually include insurance, paid vacations and holidays, pension plans, and sometimes stock-purchase plans.

Work Environment

CAD professionals almost always work in clean, quiet, well-lighted, air-conditioned offices. CAD technicians spend most of their days at a workstation. While the work does not require great physical effort, it does require patience and the ability to maintain concentration and attention for extended periods of time. Some technicians may find they suffer from eyestrain from working long periods in front of a video display screen.

CAD technicians, because of their training and experience, are valuable employees. They are called upon to exercise independent judgment and to be responsible for valuable equipment. Out of necessity, they also sometimes find themselves carrying out routine, uncomplicated tasks. CAD technicians must be able to respond well to both kinds of demands. Most CAD technicians work as part of a team. They are required to follow orders, and may encounter situations in which their individual contributions are not fully recognized. Successful CAD technicians are those who work well as team members and who can derive satisfaction from the accomplishments of the team as a whole.

Outlook

The U.S. Department of Labor predicts that the employment outlook for drafters will grow more slowly than the average for all other occupations through 2008. The best opportunities will be available to those who have skill and experience using CAD systems. Many companies in the near future will feel pressures to increase productivity in design and manufacturing activities, and CAD technology provides some of the best opportunities to improve that productivity. By some estimates, there will be as many as a million jobs available for technically trained personnel in the field of CAD/CAM technology in the next few years.

Another factor that will create a demand for CAD drafters and technicians is the continued focus on safety and quality throughout manufacturing and industrial industries. In order to do business or continue to do business with leading manufacturers, companies and lower-tier suppliers must meet stringent quality guidelines. With this focus on quality as well as safety, companies are scrutinizing their current designs more carefully than ever, requiring more CAD work for new concepts and alterations that will create a better product.

Any economic downturn could adversely affect CAD technicians because many of the industries that they serve—such as auto manufacturing or construction—fluctuate greatly with economic swings. In any event, the best opportunities will be for drafters and technicians proficient in CAD technology who continue to learn, both in school and on the job.

Increasing productivity in the industrial design and manufacturing fields will ensure the long-term economic vitality of our nation; CAD technology is one of the most promising developments in this search for increased productivity. Knowing that they are in the forefront of this important and challenging undertaking provides CAD technicians and drafters with a good deal of pride and satisfaction.

For More Information

For information about certification, student drafting contests, and job postings, contact:

American Design and Drafting Association
PO Box 11937
Columbia, SC 29211
Tel: 803-771-0008
Email: national@adda.org
Web: http://www.adda.org/

For information about the electrical field or to find the IEEE student branch nearest you, contact:

Institute of Electrical and Electronics Engineers (IEEE)
1828 L Street, NW, Suite 1202
Washington, DC 20036-5104
Tel: 202-785-0017
Web: http://www.ieee.org/usab

For information about scholarships and grants as well as student memberships, contact:

Society of Manufacturing Engineers
International Headquarters
One SME Drive
Dearborn, MI 48121
Tel: 800-733-4763
Web: http://www.sme.org/

Electronics Engineering Technicians

	School Subjects
Computer science Mathematics Physics	

	Personal Skills
Mechanical/manipulative Technical/scientific	

	Work Environment
Primarily indoors Primarily one location	

	Minimum Education Level
High school diploma	

	Salary Range
$22,000 to $36,000 to $62,500+	

	Certification or Licensing
Voluntary	

	Outlook
About as fast as the average	

Overview

Electronics engineering technicians work with electronics engineers to design, develop, and manufacture industrial and consumer electronic equipment, including sonar, radar, and navigational equipment and computers, radios, televisions, stereos, and calculators. They are involved in fabricating, operating, testing, troubleshooting, repairing, and maintaining equipment. Those involved in the development of new electronic equipment help make changes or modifications in circuitry or other design elements.

Other electronics technicians inspect newly installed equipment or instruct and supervise lower-grade technicians' installation, assembly, or repair activities.

As part of their normal duties, all electronics engineering technicians set up testing equipment, conduct tests, and analyze the results; they also prepare reports, sketches, graphs, and schematic drawings to describe electronics systems and their characteristics. Their work involves the use of a variety of hand and machine tools, including such equipment as bench lathes and drills.

Depending on their area of specialization, electronics technicians may be designated by such titles as computer laboratory technicians, development instrumentation technicians, electronic communications technicians, nuclear reactor electronics technicians, engineering development technicians, or systems testing laboratory technicians.

History

Strictly speaking, electronics technology deals with the behavior of electrons as they pass through gases, liquids, solids, and vacuums. Originally this field was an outgrowth of electrical engineering, an area concerned with the movement of electrons along conductors. As the field of electronics has expanded in scope, however, so has its definition, and today the term encompasses all areas of technology concerned with the behavior of electrons in electronic devices and equipment, including electrical engineering.

Although the field of electronics had its most spectacular growth and development during the 20th century, it is actually the product of more than 200 years of study and experiment. One of the important early experimenters in this field was Benjamin Franklin (1706-1790). His experiments with lightning and his theory that electrical charges are present in all matter influenced the thinking and established much of the vocabulary of the researchers who came after him.

The invention of the electric battery, or voltaic pile, by the Italian scientist Alessandro Volta (1745-1827) in 1800, ushered in a century of significant discoveries in the field of electricity and magnetism. Researchers working throughout Europe and the United States made important breakthroughs in how to strengthen, control, and measure the flow of electrons moving through vacuums. In the late 19th and early 20th centuries, these experiments culminated in Sir Joseph John Thomson's (1892-1975) description and measurement of the particle now called the electron.

During the early years of the 20th century, further discoveries along these lines were made by experimenters such as Lee De Forest (1873-1961) and Vladimir Zworykin (1889-1982). These discoveries led the way to developing equipment and techniques for long-distance broadcasting of radio and television signals. It was the outbreak of World War II, however, with its needs for long-distance communications equipment and, ultimately, missile-guidance systems, that brought about the rapid expansion of electronics technology and the creation of the electronics industry.

As the field of electronics technology turned to the creation of consumer and industrial products following the end of the war, its growth was spurred by two new technological developments. The first was the completion in 1946 of the first all-purpose, all-electronic digital computer. This machine, crude as it was, could handle mathematical calculations a thousand times faster than the electromechanical calculating machines of its day. Since 1946, there has been a steady growth in the speed, sophistication, and versatility of computers.

The second important development was the invention of the transistor in 1948. The transistor provided an inexpensive and compact replacement for the vacuum tubes used in nearly all electronic equipment up until then. Transistors allowed for the miniaturization of electronic circuits and were especially crucial in the development of the computer and in opening new possibilities in industrial automation.

Discoveries during the 1960s in the fields of microcircuitry and integrated circuitry led to the development of microminiaturized and more sophisticated electronic equipment, from pocket calculators, digital watches, and microwave ovens to high-speed computers and the long-range guidance systems used in spaceflights.

By the 1970s, electronics had become one of the largest industries and most important areas of technology in the industrialized world, which, in turn, has come to rely on instantaneous worldwide communications, computer-controlled or computer-assisted industrial operations, and the wide-ranging forms of electronic data processing made possible by electronics technology.

Throughout the growth and development of the electronics field, there has been a need for skilled assistants in the laboratory, on the factory floor, and in the wide variety of settings where electronic equipment is used. Electronics engineering technicians fill this important role, and will continue to do so as the electronics industry continues its rapid growth.

The Job

Most electronics technicians work in one of three broad areas of electronics: product development, manufacturing and production, or service and maintenance. Technicians involved with service and maintenance are known as *electronics service technicians*. In the product-development area, electronics technicians, or *electronics development technicians*, work directly with engineers or as part of a research team. Engineers draw up blueprints for a new product, and technicians build a prototype according to specifications. Using hand tools and small machine tools, they construct complex parts, components, and subassemblies.

After the prototype is completed, technicians work with engineers to test the product and make necessary modifications. They conduct physical and electrical tests to test the product's performance in various stressful conditions; for example, they test to see how a component will react in extreme heat and cold. Tests are run using complicated instruments and equipment, and detailed, accurate records are kept of the tests performed.

Electronics technicians in the product-development field may make suggestions for improvements in the design of a device. They may also have to construct, install, modify, or repair laboratory test equipment.

Electronics drafting is a field of electronics technology closely related to product development. *Electronics drafters,* or *computer-aided design drafters,* convert rough sketches and written or verbal information provided by engineers and scientists into easily understandable schematic, layout, or wiring diagrams to be used in manufacturing the product. These drafters may also prepare a list of components and equipment needed for producing the final product, as well as bills for materials.

Another closely related field is cost estimating. *Cost-estimating technicians* review new product proposals in order to determine the approximate total cost to produce a product. They estimate the costs for all labor, equipment, and materials needed to manufacture the product. The sales department uses these figures to determine at what price a product can be sold and whether production is economically feasible.

In the manufacturing and production phase, the electronics technicians, who are also called *electronics manufacturing and production technicians,* work in a wide variety of capacities, generally with the day-to-day handling of production problems, schedules, and costs. These technicians deal with any problems arising from the production process. They install, maintain, and repair assembly- or test-line machinery. In quality control, they inspect and test products at various stages in the production process. When a problem is discovered, they are involved in determining the nature and extent of it and in suggesting remedies.

Those involved in quality control inspect and test the products at various stages of completion. They also maintain and calibrate test equipment used in all phases of the manufacturing. They determine the causes for rejection of parts or equipment by assembly-line inspectors and then analyze field and manufacturing reports of product failures.

These technicians may make specific recommendations to their supervisors to eliminate the causes of rejects and may even suggest design, manufacturing, and process changes and establish quality-acceptance levels. They may interpret quality-control standards to the manufacturing supervisors. And they may establish and maintain quality limits on items purchased from other manufacturers, thus ensuring the quality of parts used in the equipment being assembled.

Another area of electronics technology is that of technical writing and editing. *Technical writers* and *technical editors* compile, write, and edit a wide variety of technical information. This includes instructional leaflets, operating manuals, books, and installation and service manuals having to do with the products of the company. To do this, they must confer with design and development engineers, production personnel, salespeople, drafters, and others to obtain the necessary information to prepare the text, drawings, diagrams, parts, lists, and illustrations. They must understand thoroughly how and why the equipment works in order to be able to tell the customer how to use it and the service technician how to install and service it.

At times, technical writers and editors may help prepare technical reports and proposals and write technical articles for engineering societies, management, and other associations. Their job is to produce the means (through printed word and pictures) by which the customer can get the most value out of the purchased equipment.

Requirements

High School

A high school diploma is necessary for anyone wishing to build a career as an electronics engineering technician. While in high school, you should take algebra, geometry, physics, chemistry, computer science, English, and communications classes. Courses in electronics and introductory electricity are also helpful as are shop courses and courses in mechanical drawing.

Postsecondary Training

Most employers prefer to hire graduates of two-year postsecondary training programs. These programs provide a solid foundation in the basics of electronics and supply enough general background in science as well as other career-related fields such as business and economics to aid the student in advancing to positions of greater responsibility.

Two-year programs in electronics technology are available at community colleges and technical institutes. Completion of these programs results in an associate's degree. Programs vary quite a bit, but in general, a typical first-year curriculum includes courses in physics for electronics, technical mathematics, communications, AC/DC circuit analysis, electronic amplifiers, transistors, and instruments and measurements.

Typical second-year courses include physics, applied electronics, computer information systems, electronic drafting, electronic instruments and measurements, communications circuits and systems, digital electronics, technical writing, and control circuits and systems.

Students unable to attend a technical institute or community college should not overlook opportunities provided by the military. The military provides extensive training in electronics and other related fields. In addition, some major companies, particularly utilities, hire people straight out of high school and train them through in-house programs. Other companies promote people to technicians' positions from lower-level positions, provided they attend educational workshops and classes sponsored by the company.

Certification or Licensing

Voluntary certification as a certified electronics technician (CET) is obtained by many technicians. This certification is regarded as a demonstration of professional dedication, determination, and know-how. CET certification is available through professional associations (see addresses at the end of this article) and is awarded to those who successfully complete a written multiple-choice examination. The associate-level CET test is designed for technicians with less than four years of experience. After four years of experience or education, a technician can take another CET examination in order to earn a journeyman-level CET certification. Additional certificates are available based on proficiency and experience in different areas.

Other Requirements

Prospective electronics technicians should have an interest in and an aptitude for mathematics and science and should enjoy using tools and scientific equipment; on the personal side, they should be patient, methodical, persistent, and able to get along with different kinds of people. Because technology changes so rapidly, technicians will need to pursue additional training throughout their careers. A person planning to work in electronics needs to have the ability and desire to learn quickly, an inquisitive mind, and the willingness to read and study materials to keep up-to-date.

Exploring

If you are interested in a career as an electronics engineering technician, you can gain relevant experience by taking shop courses, belonging to electronics or radio clubs in school, and assembling electronic equipment with commercial kits.

You should take every opportunity to discuss the field with people working in it. Try to visit a variety of different kinds of electronics facilities—service shops, manufacturing plants, and research laboratories—either through individual visits or through field trips organized by teachers or guidance counselors. These visits will provide a realistic idea of the opportunities in the different areas of the electronics industry. You should also take an introductory course in basic electricity or electronics to test your aptitude, skills, and interest. If you enroll in a community college or technical school, you may be able to secure off-quarter or part-time internships with local employers through your school's job placement office. Internships are valuable ways to gain experience while still in school.

Employers

Electronics engineering technicians are employed by companies that design, develop, and manufacture industrial and consumer electronic equipment. Such employers include service shops, manufacturing plants, and research laboratories.

Starting Out

Students may find their first full-time positions through their schools' job placement offices. These offices tend to develop very good working relationships with area employers and can offer students excellent interviewing opportunities.

Another way to obtain employment is through direct contact with a particular company. It is best to write to the personnel department and include a resume summarizing one's education and experience. If the company has an appropriate opening, a company representative will schedule an interview for the prospective employee. There are also many excellent public and commercial employment organizations that can help graduates obtain jobs appropriate to their training and experience. In addition, the classified ads in most metropolitan Sunday newspapers list a number of job openings with companies in the area.

Professional associations compile information on job openings and publish job lists. For example, the International Society of Certified Electronics Technicians (ISCET) publishes a monthly job list, titled *Career Opportunities in Electronics*, which lists job openings around the country. Information about job openings can also be found in trade magazines on electronics.

Advancement

Advancement possibilities in the field of electronics are almost unlimited. Technicians usually begin work under the direct and constant supervision of an experienced technician, scientist, or engineer. As they gain experience or additional education, they are given more responsible assignments, often carrying out particular work programs under only very general supervision. From there, technicians may move into supervisory positions; those with exceptional ability can sometimes qualify for professional positions after receiving additional academic training.

The following short paragraphs describe some of the positions to which electronics technicians can advance.

Electronics technician supervisors work on more complex projects than do electronics technicians. They supervise other technicians and may also have administrative duties, such as making the employee work schedule, assigning laboratory projects to various technicians, overseeing the training progress of new employees, and keeping the workplace clean, organized, and well stocked. In general, they tend to have more direct contact with project managers and project engineers.

Engineering technicians are senior technicians or engineering assistants who work as part of a team of engineers and technicians in research and development of new products. Additional education, resulting in a bachelor of science degree in engineering, is required for this position.

Production test supervisors make detailed analyses of production assembly lines in order to determine where production tests should be placed along the line and the nature and goal of the tests. They may be responsible for designing the equipment setup used in production testing.

Quality control supervisors determine the scope of a product sampling and the kinds of tests to be run on production units. They translate specifications into testing procedures.

Workers who want to advance to engineering positions can become *electrical engineers* or *electronics engineers* through additional education. A bachelor of science degree in engineering is required.

All electronics technicians will need to pursue additional training throughout their careers in order to keep up-to-date with new technologies and techniques. Many employers offer continuing education in the form of in-house workshops or outside seminars. Professional associations also offer seminars and classes on newer technologies and skill building.

Earnings

Engineering technicians who have completed a two-year postsecondary training program and are working in private industry earn salaries of approximately $27,680 to $45,750 a year, according to the *Occupational Outlook Handbook*. Average yearly earnings of all engineering technicians were approximately $35,970 in 1998. At the very top pay levels, technicians in supervisory positions or with considerable experience can earn $62,540 or higher.

Electronics engineering technicians generally receive premium pay for overtime work on Sundays and holidays and for evening and night-shift work. Most employers offer benefit packages that include paid holidays, paid vacations, sick days, and health insurance. Companies may also offer pension and retirement plans, profit sharing, 401-K plans, tuition assistance programs, and release time for additional education.

Work Environment

Because electronic equipment usually must be manufactured in a dust-free, climate-controlled environment, electronics engineering technicians can expect to work in modern, comfortable, well-lighted surroundings. Many electronics plants have been built in industrial parks with ample parking and little traffic congestion. Technicians who work with cable, MATV, satellites, and antennas work outside. Frequency of injuries in the electronics industry is far less than in most other industries, and injuries that do occur are usually not serious.

Most employees work a 40-hour workweek, although overtime is not unusual. Some technicians regularly average 50 to 60 hours a week.

Some workers in electronics manufacturing are covered by union agreements. The principal unions involved are the International Union of Electronics, Electrical, Salaried, Machine, and Furniture Workers; the International Brotherhood of Electrical Workers; the International Association of Machinists and Aerospace Workers; and the United Electrical, Radio, and Machine Workers of America.

Outlook

There is good reason to believe that the electronics industry will remain one of the most important industries in the United States through the next decade. Consumer products such as large screen and high-definition televisions, videocassette recorders, compact disc players, personal computers, and home appliances with solid-state controls are constantly evolving and in high demand. Two areas showing high growth are computers and telecommunications products. Multimedia and interactive products are expanding rapidly, and many new products are expected in the coming years. In addition, increasing automation and computer-assisted manufacturing processes rely on advanced electronic technology.

All of these uses for electronics should continue to stimulate growth in the electronics industry. The U.S. Department of Labor estimates that opportunities for electronics engineering technicians will increase as fast as the average through 2008. Foreign competition, general economic conditions, and levels of government spending may affect certain areas of the field to some degree. This is an industry, however, that is becoming so central to our lives and for which there is still such growth potential that it seems unlikely that any single factor could substantially curb its growth and its need for specially trained personnel.

Prospective electronics technicians should begin paying attention to certain factors that might affect the areas in which they are thinking of working. For example, workers planning to work for the military or for a military contractor or subcontractor in radar technology need to keep an eye on federal legislation concerning military spending cuts or increases. The Department of Defense has cut orders for many of the products that it ordered in large quantities in the past. This is having a significant impact on some areas of electronics production.

In some areas, the demand for workers is higher than the number of trained workers available. For example, there is a need for highly skilled electronics technicians at companies that produce electronics products with related telecommunications or computer technology. Electromedical and biomedical subfields dealing with technical hospital machines have also been identified as high-demand areas.

The electronics industry is undeniably indispensable to our lives, and although there will be fluctuations in growth for certain subfields, there will be a need for qualified personnel in others. The key to success for an electronics technician is to stay up-to-date with technology and to be professionally versatile. Building a career on a solid academic and hands-on foundation in basic electronics enables an electronics technician to remain competitive in the job market.

For More Information

For information on careers and educational programs, contact:

Institute of Electrical and Electronics Engineers
1828 L Street, NW, Suite 1202
Washington, DC 20036-5104
Tel: 202-785-0017
Web: http://www.ieee.org

Electronic Industries Alliance
2500 Wilson Boulevard
Arlington, VA 22201-3834
Tel: 703-907-7500
Web: http://www.eia.org

For information on student chapters and certification, contact:

International Society of Certified Electronics Technicians
2708 West Berry Street
Fort Worth, TX 76109
Tel: 817-921-9101
Email: iscetFW@aol.com
Web: http://www.iscet.org

For information on careers, educational programs, and certification, contact:

Electronics Technicians Association
602 North Jackson
Greencastle, IN 46135
Tel: 765-653-4301
Email: eta@indy.tdsnet.com
Web: http://www.eta-sda.com

American Society of Certified Engineering Technicians
PO Box 1348
Flowery Branch, GA 30542
Tel: 770-967-9173

For information on student clubs, careers, and educational programs, contact:

Junior Engineering Technical Society, Inc.
1420 King Street, Suite 405
Alexandria, VA 22314
Tel: 703-548-5387
Email: jets@nae.edu
Web: http://www.jets.org/

Fiber Optics Technicians

School Subjects	Technical/Shop
Personal Skills	Mechanical/manipulative Technical/scientific
Work Environment	Indoors and outdoors Primarily multiple locations
Minimum Education Level	High school diploma
Salary Range	$26,779 to $29,902 to $36,857
Certification or Licensing	Voluntary
Outlook	Faster than the average

Overview

Fiber optics technicians work with the optical fibers and cables used in transmitting communications data. Depending on the area of employment, technicians splice fibers, fuse fibers together, and install fiber cables beneath ground and in buildings. These technicians work for telephone and cable companies, and other businesses involved in telecommunications.

History

A need to convey messages quickly led to experimentation in the use of light to communicate. Before the introduction of the electric telegraph in the mid-1800s, a series of semaphores atop towers allowed for communication between tower operators. Ships also used light signals to communicate with each other. But the reliability of wires to carry electricity, and the invention of the electric telegraph and the telephone, put the further development of optical communications on hold.

Studies in the field of medicine led to the discovery that rods of glass or plastic could carry light. In the 1950s, these developments helped such engineers as Alec Reeves of Great Britain in the experimentation of fiber optics for telecommunications. High television and telephone use demanded more transmission bandwidth, and the invention of the laser in 1960 made optical communications a reality. Technical barriers remained, however, and experimentation continued for many years, leading to the first telephone field trials in 1977. Today, the career of fiber optics technician is one of the fastest growing, as telecommunications companies recognize the importance of fiber optics in the future of high-speed, high-definition service. Most phone connections made today are over fiber optic cables. The Internet is also transmitted by fiber optics.

The Job

As a fiber optics technician, you'll prepare, install, and test fiber optics transmission systems. These systems are composed of fiber optic cables and allow for data communication between computers, phones, and faxes. When working for a telecommunications company, you'll often be required to install lines for local area networks (LAN)—these data networks serve small areas of linked computers, such as in an office.

The telecommunications company for which you work will contract with a company to create a communications system. A salesman will evaluate the customer's need, then order the materials for the installation. You'll take these materials to the job site. Each job site may be very different—you may be working in a variety of different locales. First, you'll need to get a sense of the area. You'll walk through with the client, evaluating the areas where you'll be installing fiber optic cable. Newer buildings will be readily equipped for installation; in some older buildings, it may be more difficult to get behind ceiling tiles and in the walls.

After you've readied the area for cable, you will then run the cable from the computer's mainframe to individual workstations. You'll then test the cable, using power meters and other devices, by running a laser through it. Your equipment measures the amount of time it takes for the laser to go through, determining any signal loss or faults in the fiber link.

You may also be fusing fibers together. This involves cleaning the fiber and cutting it with a special diamond-headed cleaver. After you've prepared both ends, you'll place them into a fusion splicer. At the press of a button, the splicer fuses the two fibers together.

Requirements

High School

There aren't really any specific high school courses that will prepare you for work as a fiber optics technician, but shop classes will give you experience working with tools to complete a variety of projects, and speech and writing classes will help you improve your communication skills.

Postsecondary Training

A college degree isn't required, but can give you an edge when looking for work as a fiber optics technician. A number of community colleges across the country offer programs in fiber optics technology or broadband networks technology. These programs offer such courses as cable construction, fiber optic installation techniques, singlemode and multimode systems, and wavelength and bandwidth. They also may include lab and certification components. Short-term training opportunities, lasting only a few days, may also be available at some schools.

Certification or Licensing

Certification isn't required of fiber optics technicians, but may be available from local community colleges and training programs. The Fiber Optic Association (FOA) offers national certification; there are currently over 500 fiber optics technicians certified by FOA.

Other Requirements

Because of the fine nature of the fibers, you should have a steady hand and good eyesight in assembling fiber optic cables. You'll also need good math skills for working with detailed plans and designs. Some companies may require you to have your own special fiber optic tools.

Exploring

Ask a teacher to set up an interview with an experienced fiber optics technician. Talking with someone in the field is the best way to learn the pros and cons of any career.

Employers

Fiber optics technicians work for telephone companies, cable companies, and computer networking businesses. They may also work freelance, hiring on with companies on special installation projects.

Starting Out

There are a great many sources of information about developments in fiber optics and the telecommunications industry, including *Fiber Optic Product News Online* (http://www.fpnmag.com), which features employment opportunities. When you complete a fiber optics technology program, your school will be able to direct you to local job opportunities. Information Gatekeepers publishes a fiber optics career directory listing over 1,000 companies. You can contact Information Gatekeepers at 800-323-1088.

Advancement

Even without special fiber optics training, you may be able to enter the job market in an entry level position with a telecommunications company. The company may have its own training program, or may pay for you to attend seminars in fiber optics technology. After you've gained experience working with fiber optic cable, you may be able to move into a management or executive position. You could also become a consultant, advising companies on data transmission problems.

Earnings

The Women in Cable and Telecommunications Foundation and Cablevision Magazine conducted a survey in 1998 to examine salary parities between men and women in the telecommunications industry. In entry level professional/technical positions, men had average annual salaries of $26,779 and women had salaries of $26,034. (76 percent of the male respondents were technicians, while none of the female respondents were.) At the associate level, men made $29,902 a year, while women made $31,133. (66 percent of the men were technicians; 6.5 percent of the women.) At the senior level, men averaged $36,857 and women averaged $36,803. (46 percent of the men were technicians; 7.1 percent of the women.)

Companies offer a variety of benefit packages, which can include any of the following: paid holidays, vacations, and sick days; personal days; medical, dental, and life insurance; profit-sharing plans; 401-K plans; retirement and pension plans; and educational assistance programs.

Work Environment

If working as an assembler, you'll spend most of your time sitting at a bench. As an installer, you'll be out in the field. Though you may be installing the fibers beneath ground, you'll have machinery to do most of the digging of trenches. Part of your time will be spent outside repairing fiber, and part of your time will be spent in a van preparing the fibers for installation. You may also be installing fiber cables in buildings; this will require some climbing of ladders and working beneath floorboards.

Outlook

Digital transmissions will soon be the norm for telecommunications—not only do modern offices require data communications systems, but cable companies are investing in fiber optics to offer digital TV, as well as quality phone service. Also, the cost of fiber is dropping, which means more companies will invest in fiber optics. As a result, experienced fiber optics assemblers and installers will find plenty of job opportunities.

For More Information

To learn about telecommunications technology and the number of uses for fiber optics, visit the OSA Web site:

Optical Society of America (OSA)
2010 Massachusetts Avenue, NW
Washington, DC 20036
Tel: 202-223-8130
Web: http://www.osa.org/

To learn about certification and training opportunities, contact:

The Fiber Optic Association
Box 230851
Boston, MA 02123-0851
Tel: 617-469-2362
Web: http://world.std.com/~foa/

Fluid Power Technicians

	School Subjects
Mathematics Technical/Shop	
	Personal Skills
Mechanical/manipulative Technical/scientific	
	Work Environment
Primarily indoors Primarily multiple locations	
	Minimum Education Level
Some postsecondary training	
	Salary Range
$22,000 to $33,000 to $40,000+	
	Certification or Licensing
Voluntary	
	Outlook
Faster than the average	

Overview

Fluid power technicians deal with equipment that utilizes the pressure of a liquid or gas in a closed container to transmit, multiply, or control power. Working under the supervision of an engineer or engineering staff, they assemble, install, maintain, and test fluid power equipment, which is found in almost every facet of American daily life.

History

Machinery that operates on fluid power has been used for thousands of years. In Roman times, water flowing past a rotating paddle wheel was used to produce power for milling. Early leather bellows, hand-operated by blacksmiths, were the first known devices to use compressed air. In Italy, in the 16th century, a more sophisticated bellows was invented that used falling water to compress air. Shortly thereafter, Denis Papin, a French physicist, used power from a waterwheel to compress air in a similar manner.

The 19th century brought the first practical application of an air-driven, piston-operated hammer, invented in Great Britain by George Law. In the mid-1800s, water-cooled reciprocating compressors were introduced in the United States and resulted in the development of large compressed-air units that factory workers used to operate industrial tools. In 1875, American engineer and industrialist George Westinghouse created and utilized a continuous automatic compressed-air brake system for trains.

In the latter part of the 19th century and the early part of the 20th, experiments in fluid dynamics by Osborne Reynolds and Ludwig Prandtl led to a new understanding of the way fluid behaves in certain circumstances. These findings laid the groundwork for modern fluid power mechanics. The 20th century has witnessed a significant increase in the use of fluid power for many different uses.

Fluid power workers are now employed in any number of industries, from aerospace to materials handling. Fluid power is also routinely used and depended upon in almost everyone's daily life. Anyone who has ever ridden in a car, for example, has relied upon fluid power to operate its hydraulic braking system. With fluid power so widely used, literally thousands of businesses throughout the United States employ men and women who are trained in its various aspects. Fluid power technicians, with their specialized skills and knowledge, have become a mainstay of industrial support groups that work with this type of machinery.

The Job

Many different machines use some kind of fluid power system, including equipment used in industries such as agriculture, manufacturing, defense, and mining. We come across fluid power systems every day when we use automatic door closers, bicycle pumps, and spray guns. Even automobile transmissions incorporate fluid power.

There are two types of fluid power machines. The first kind—hydraulic machines—use water, oil, or another liquid in a closed system to transmit the energy needed to do work. For example, a hydraulic jack, which can be used to lift heavy loads, is a cylinder with a piston fitted inside it. When a liquid is pumped into the bottom of the cylinder, the piston is forced upward, lifting the weight on the jack. To lower the weight, the liquid is released through a valve, returning the pressure in the system to normal.

Pneumatic machines, the other type of fluid power systems, are activated by the pressure of air or another gas in a closed system. Pavement-breaking jackhammers and compressed-air paint sprayers are common examples of pneumatic machines.

Fluid power systems are a part of most machines used in industry, so fluid power technicians work in many different settings. Most often, however, they work in factories where fluid power systems are used in manufacturing. In such a factory, for example, they might maintain and service pneumatic machines that bolt together products on an automated assembly line.

In their work, fluid power technicians analyze blueprints, drawings, and specifications; set up various milling, shaping, grinding, and drilling machines, and make precision parts; use sensitive measuring instruments to make sure the parts are exactly the required size; and use hand and power tools to put together components of the fluid power system they are assembling or repairing.

Technicians may also be responsible for testing fluid power systems. To determine whether a piece of equipment is working properly, they connect the unit to test equipment that measures such factors as fluid pressure, flow rates, and power loss from friction or wear. Based on their analysis of the test results, they may advise changes in the equipment setup or instrumentation.

Some technicians work for companies that are researching better ways to develop and use fluid power systems. They may work in laboratories as part of research and development teams who set up fluid power equipment and test it under operating conditions. Other technicians work as sales and service representatives for companies that make and sell fluid power equipment to industrial plants. These technicians travel from one plant to another, providing customers with specialized information and assistance with their equipment. Some technicians repair and maintain fluid power components of heavy equipment used in construction, on farms, or in mining. Because fluid power technology is important in the flight controls, landing gear, and brakes of airplanes, many technicians are also employed in the aircraft industry.

Requirements

High School

If you are considering a career in fluid power, you should take as many courses as possible in computer science and mathematics. Physics, shop, drafting, and English will also provide a solid background for this type of work.

Postsecondary Training

In the past, you could become a fluid power technician with only a high school diploma and, perhaps, some related technical experience. Technicians were trained in fluid power technology by their employers or by taking short courses or workshops. Today, however, most employers prefer to hire fluid power technicians who have at least two years of post-high school training, such as that offered by community and technical colleges.

There are relatively few technical training programs that focus primarily on fluid power technology—fewer than 30 in the entire United States. A student enrolled in one of these programs might expect to take classes on very specialized topics, such as fluid power math, process and fabrication fundamentals, hydraulic components and accessories, pneumatic components and circuits, and advanced systems calculations. If it is not possible to attend one of the schools that offer programs in fluid power, training in a related field, such as mechanical or electrical technology, can provide adequate preparation for employment.

Certification or Licensing

Certification for fluid power technicians is voluntary. Offered through the Fluid Power Certification Board, the certification process is administered by the Fluid Power Society. Applicants must attend two or more days of classes and pass a written, three-hour examination before receiving technician certification. This certification may be beneficial to technicians in finding jobs, obtaining more advanced positions, or receiving higher pay.

Other Requirements

Technicians must be able to understand and analyze mechanical systems. In order to do this well, they should have both mechanical aptitude and an analytical mindset. Because they often work on teams, an ability to work well and communicate easily with others is important. Finally, a successful technician should enjoy challenges and the troubleshooting of problems.

Exploring

School or public libraries should have books that explain the field of fluid power. If students happen to live near one of the schools that offers a degree in fluid power technology, it may be possible to arrange a meeting with instructors or students in the program. Talking with someone who is already employed as a fluid power technician can be an excellent way of learning about the job firsthand. Finally, taking certain classes, such as machine shop, physics, or electronics, might help prospective technicians gauge their enjoyment and ability level for this work.

Employers

The largest consumers of fluid power products are the aerospace, construction equipment, agricultural equipment, machine tools, and materials handling industries, according to the National Fluid Power Association, an industry trade organization. Fluid power also provides power for auxiliary systems on planes, ships, trains, and trucks.

Starting Out

Most fluid power technicians obtain their jobs through their community and technical college placement offices. In addition, organizations such as the Fluid Power Society and the Fluid Power Educational Foundation have lists of their corporate members that can be used to start a job search. Some openings might be listed in the employment sections of newspapers.

Advancement

Some technicians advance simply by becoming more knowledgeable and skilled in their work and eventually receive more responsibility. Another route for technicians is to become a *fluid power specialist* by taking additional training and upgrading their certification. A specialist designs and applies systems, and can instruct newer employees on the basics of fluid power systems.

Some technicians go into sales and marketing, using their experience and knowledge to provide customers with technical assistance. Another option is to become a *fluid power consultant*, who works with different companies to analyze, design, or improve fluid power systems.

Earnings

The average starting salary for fluid power technicians varies according to geographic location and industry, but technical colleges estimate $22,000 per year. An estimated national average wage for technicians might be in the low to mid-$30,000s. Those who move into consulting or other advanced positions can earn even more. Most workers in this field receive a full benefits package, often including vacation days, sick leave, medical and life insurance, and a retirement plan.

Work Environment

Because fluid power technicians work in any number of different industries, their work environments vary. Many work in industrial settings and must spend much of their time on the manufacturing floor. In this case, they may have to become accustomed to noise and heat generated by the machinery, although the industry is addressing the noise level issue. Others work in laboratories or testing facilities. Those involved in sales and marketing or in installing and repairing equipment may travel to different customer locations.

The work is frequently dirty, as technicians often have to handle machinery that has been used and may be leaking fluid. Also, working on large machinery and components requires physical strength and may require being in areas where safety regulations must be followed.

Many workers in this field find their jobs enjoyable and satisfying. Because they deal with different problems and solutions all the time, the work is challenging, interesting, and not repetitious. It can also be gratifying to figure out how to make a machine run properly or improve upon its performance through testing and experimenting.

Outlook

Because fluid power is used in so many different industries, the need for technicians is growing rapidly. Currently, in fact, the demand for these trained workers exceeds the supply. In the 1990s, electrohydraulic and electropneumatic technologies opened up new markets, such as active suspensions on automobiles, and reestablished older markets such as robotics. Therefore, the fluid power industry is expected to continue growing and the outlook for technicians should remain excellent through 2008.

For More Information

For information about certification, contact:

Fluid Power Certification Board Secretariat
2433 North Mayfair Road, Suite 111
Milwaukee, WI 53226
Tel: 414-257-0910
Web: http://www.ifps.org/certific.html

For a list of schools offering courses in fluid power technology and information about available scholarships, contact:

Fluid Power Educational Foundation
3333 North Mayfair Road, Suite 101
Milwaukee, WI 53222
Tel: 414-778-3364
Web: http://www.fpef.org

For information about the fluid power industry, contact:

National Fluid Power Association
3333 North Mayfair Road
Milwaukee, WI 53222-3219
Tel: 414-778-3344
Web: http://www.nfpa.com

Industrial Engineering Technicians

School Subjects
Computer science
Mathematics

Personal Skills
Communication/ideas
Technical/scientific

Work Environment
Primarily indoors
Primarily one location

Minimum Education Level
Associate's degree

Salary Range
$22,300 to $38,400 to $59,800

Certification or Licensing
Voluntary

Outlook
About as fast as the average

Overview

Industrial engineering technicians assist industrial engineers in their duties: they collect and analyze data and make recommendations for the efficient use of personnel, materials, and machines to produce goods or to provide services. They may study the time, movements, and methods a worker uses to accomplish daily tasks in production, maintenance, or clerical areas.

Industrial engineering technicians prepare charts to illustrate work flow, floor layouts, materials handling, and machine utilization. They make statistical studies, analyze production costs, prepare layouts of machinery and equipment, help plan work flow and work assignments, and recommend revisions to revamp production methods or improve standards. As part of their job, industrial engineering technicians often use equipment such as computers, timers, and camcorders.

History

Industrial engineering is a direct outgrowth of the Industrial Revolution, which began in England in the 18th century and later spread to the United States. By linking a power source, such as a steam engine, to simple mechanical devices, early mechanical and industrial engineers were able to design and build factories to rapidly and economically produce textiles, clothing, and other materials.

Today, factories in the United States and around the world produce almost all of our consumer goods. This tremendous growth led to a need for industrial engineers, who evaluate not only the machines that go into the factory but also the raw materials, the people who run the machines, the costs and efficiency of operations, and other factors that affect the success of an industrial operation.

Industrial engineering as a separate specialty emerged during the 20th century. For as long as there have been industrial engineers, however, there have been skilled assistants who work with them and handle tasks that do not require the engineer's direct involvement. Today's industrial engineering technicians are the direct descendants of those assistants. As the years have gone by, the number, variety, and complexity of the responsibilities falling to industrial engineering technicians have increased greatly. In the past, assistants could rely purely on common sense and on-the-job experience, but today's industrial engineering technicians must be specially trained and educated before entering the workplace.

Today, the scope of industrial engineering goes far beyond the factory. The principles of work flow and quality control are now applied to other work environments, including corporations' offices and retail stores. The industrial engineering technician is recognized and respected as a team member in evaluating and improving production and working conditions.

The Job

The type of work done by an industrial engineering technician depends on the location, size, and products of the company for which he or she works. Usually a technician's duties fall into one or more of the following areas: work measurement, production control, wage and job evaluation, quality control, or plant layout.

Industrial engineering technicians involved in methods engineering analyze new and existing products to determine the best way to make them at the lowest cost. In these analyses, *methods engineering technicians* recommend which processing equipment to use; determine how fast materials can be processed; develop flowcharts; and consider all materials-handling, movement, and storage aspects of the production.

The *materials-handling technician* studies the current methods of handling material, then compares and evaluates alternatives. The technician will suggest changes that reduce physical effort, make handling safer, and lower costs and damage to products.

Work measurement technicians study the production rate of a given product and determine how much time is needed for all the activities involved. They do this by timing the motions necessary for a complete operation, analyzing tapes of workers, and consulting historical statistics collected in the factory. *Time study technicians* analyze and determine elements of work, their order, and the time required to produce a part.

The engineering technicians in production control often work in scheduling departments, where they coordinate many complex details to ensure product delivery on a specified date. To do this, *production control technicians* must know the products and assemblies to be made, the routes to be used through the plant, and the time required for the process. These technicians also issue orders to manufacture products, check machine loads, and maintain constant surveillance of the master schedules.

Production control technicians also work in dispatching offices, where they issue orders to the production areas, watch department machine loads, report progress of products, and expedite the delivery of needed parts to avoid delays.

Inventory control technicians maintain inventories of raw materials, semi-finished products, completed products, packaging materials, and supplies. They ensure an adequate supply of raw materials, watch for obsolete parts, and prevent damage or loss to products.

In quality control, technicians work with inspection departments to maintain quality standards set by production engineers. They check all incoming materials and forecast the quality of obtainable materials. *Quality control technicians* use a variety of techniques and perform other duties that include part-drawing surveillance, checking of parts with inspection tools, identifying trouble, and providing corrective procedures.

Cost control technicians compare actual product costs with budgeted allowances. These technicians investigate cost discrepancies, offer corrective measures, and analyze results.

Budget technicians gather figures and facts to project and graph break-even points. They help prepare budgets for management and present the effects of production schedules on profitability.

Technicians working in the area of wage and job evaluation gather and organize information pertaining to the skill, manual effort, education, and other factors involved in the jobs of all hourly employees. This information helps to set salary ranges and establish job descriptions.

The *plant layout technician* works with materials-handling personnel, supervisors, and management to help make alterations in manufacturing facilities. These technicians study old floor plans; consider all present and future aspects of operations; and revise, consult, and then propose layouts to production and management personnel.

Requirements

High School

Prospective industrial engineering technicians should take classes in algebra, geometry, calculus, chemistry, physics, trigonometry, and English. Mechanical drawing, metal shop, and communications would also be helpful. Computers have become the most used tool in industrial engineering, so computer science classes are critical to a student considering a career in this field. Also recommended are courses in shop sketching, blueprint reading, mechanical drawing, and model making, if available.

Postsecondary Training

Most employers prefer to hire someone with at least a two-year degree in engineering technology although it is possible to qualify for some jobs with no formal training. Training is available at technical institutes, junior and community colleges, extension divisions of universities, public and private vocational-technical schools, and through some technical training programs in the armed services.

Most two-year associate programs accredited by the Accreditation Board for Engineering and Technology (ABET) include first-year courses in mathematics, orthographic and isometric sketching, blueprint reading, manufacturing processes, communications, technical reporting, introduction to numerical control, and introduction to computer-aided design (CAD).

Typical second-year courses include methods, operation, and safety engineering; industrial materials; statistics; quality control; computer control of industrial processes; plant layout and materials handling; process planning and manufacturing costs; production problems; psychology and human relations; and industrial organization and institutions. Since the type and quality of programs and schools vary considerably, prospective students are advised to consider ABET-accredited programs first.

Certification or Licensing

To give recognition and encouragement to industrial engineering technicians, the National Institute for Certification in Engineering Technologies (NICET) has established a certification program that some technicians may wish to consider. Although certification is not generally required by employers, those with certification often have a competitive advantage when it comes to hiring and promotions. Certification is available at various levels, each combining a written examination in a specialty field with a specified amount of job-related experience.

Other Requirements

Industrial engineering technicians should be adept at compiling and organizing data and be able to express themselves clearly and persuasively both orally and in writing. They should be detail oriented and enjoy solving problems.

Exploring

Opportunities to gain experience in high school are somewhat limited. However, students can obtain part-time work or summer jobs in industrial settings, even if not specifically in the industrial engineering area. Although this work may consist of menial tasks, it offers firsthand experience and demonstrates interest to future employers. Part-time jobs often lead to permanent employment, and some companies offer tuition reimbursement for educational costs.

Insights into the industrial engineering field can also be obtained in less direct ways. Professional associations regularly publish newsletters and other information relevant to the technician. Industrial firms frequently advertise or publish articles in professional journals or in business and general interest magazines that discuss innovations in plant layout, cost control, and productivity improvements. By finding and collecting these articles, prospective technicians can acquaint themselves with and stay informed on developments in the field.

Employers

Industrial engineering technicians are most often found in durable goods manufacturing, such as electronic and electrical machinery and equipment, industrial machinery and equipment, instruments, and transportation equipment. Some technicians are employed by engineering and business services companies that do contract engineering work. The U.S. Departments of Defense, Transportation, Agriculture, and Interior are also major employers, along with state and municipal governments.

Starting Out

Many industrial engineering technicians find their first jobs through interviews with company recruiters who visit campuses. In many cases, students are invited to visit the prospective employer's plant for further consultation and to become better acquainted with the area, product, and facilities. For many students, the job placement office of their college or technical school is the best source of possible jobs. Local manufacturers or companies are in constant contact with these facilities, so they have the most up-to-date job listings.

Advancement

As industrial engineering technicians gain additional experience, and especially if they pursue further education, they become candidates for advancement. Continuing education is fast becoming the most important way to advance. Many employers encourage this and will reimburse education costs.

The typical advancement path for industrial engineering technicians is to become a supervisor, an industrial engineer, or possibly a chief industrial engineer.

Here are some examples of positions to which technicians might aspire:

Production control managers supervise all production control employees, train new technicians, and coordinate manufacturing departments.

Production supervisors oversee manufacturing personnel and compare departmental records of production, scrap, and expenditures with departmental allowances.

Plant layout engineers supervise all plant-layout department personnel, estimate costs, and confer directly with other department heads to obtain information needed by the layout department.

Managers of quality control supervise all inspection and quality control employees, select techniques, teach employees new techniques, and meet with tool room and production people when manufacturing tolerances or scrap become a problem.

Chief industrial engineers supervise all industrial engineering employees, consult with department heads, direct departmental projects, set budgets, and prepare reports.

Earnings

The salary range for entry-level industrial engineering technicians varies according to the product being manufactured, geographic location, and the education and skills of the technician. According to the U.S. Bureau of Labor Statistics, the average annual salary for industrial engineering technicians in 1997 was $38,360. Some technicians, however, especially those at the very beginning of their careers, earn about $22,230 a year, while some senior technicians with special skills and experience earn over $68,720 a year. In addition to salary, most employers offer paid vacation time, holidays, insurance and retirement plans, and tuition assistance for work-related courses.

Work Environment

Industrial engineering technicians generally work indoors. Depending on their jobs, they may work in the shop or office areas or in both. The type of plant facilities depends on the product. For example, an electronics plant producing small electronic products requiring very exacting tolerances has very clean working conditions.

Industrial engineering technicians often travel to other locations or areas. They may accompany engineers to technical conventions or on visits to other companies to gain insight into new or different methods of operation and production.

Continuing education plays a large role in the life of industrial engineering technicians. They may attend classes or seminars, keeping up-to-date with emerging technology and methods of managing production efficiently.

Hours of work may vary and depend on factory shifts. Industrial engineering technicians are often asked to get jobs done quickly and to meet very tight deadlines.

Outlook

As products become more technically demanding to produce, competitive pressures will force companies to improve and update manufacturing facilities and product designs. Thus, the demand for well-trained industrial engineering technicians will stay about average through 2008. Opportunities will be best for individuals who have up-to-date skills. As technology becomes more sophisticated, employers will continue to seek technicians who require the least amount of additional job training.

The employment outlook varies with area of specialization and industry. For example, changing and increasing numbers of environmental and safety regulations may lead companies to revise some of their procedures and practices, and new technicians may be needed to assist in these changeovers. However, technicians whose jobs are defense-related may experience fewer opportunities because of recent defense cutbacks.

Prospective technicians should keep in mind that advances in technology and management techniques make industrial engineering a constantly changing field. Technicians will be able to take advantage of new opportunities only if they are willing to continue their training and education throughout their careers.

For More Information

For information about membership in a professional society specifically created for engineering technicians, contact:

American Society of Certified Engineering Technicians
PO Box 1348
Flowery Branch, GA 30542
Tel: 770-967-9173

For more information on careers and training as an industrial engineering technician, contact:

IEEE Industry Applications Society
c/o Institute of Electrical and Electronics Engineers
3 Park Avenue, 17th Floor
New York, NY 10017
Tel: 212-419-7900
Web: http://www.ieee.org/eab/

Institute of Industrial Engineers
25 Technology Park/Atlanta
Norcross, GA 30092
Tel: 404-449-0460
Web: http://www.iienet.org

For more information on careers as an engineering technician, contact:

Junior Engineering Technical Society, Inc.
1420 King Street, Suite 405
Alexandria, VA 22314-2794
Tel: 703-548-5387
Web: http://www.jets.org

For information about obtaining certification, contact:

National Institute for Certification in Engineering Technologies
1420 King Street
Alexandria, VA 22314-2715
Tel: 888-476-4238
Web: http://www.nicet.org

Instrumentation Technicians

	School Subjects
Mathematics	
Physics	
Technical/Shop	

	Personal Skills
Mechanical/manipulative	
Technical/scientific	

	Work Environment
Primarily indoors	
Primarily one location	

	Minimum Education Level
Associate's degree	

	Salary Range
$20,000 to $38,300 to $64,000	

	Certification or Licensing
Voluntary	

	Outlook
About as fast as the average	

Overview

Instrumentation technicians are skilled craftsworkers who do precision work and are involved in the field of measurement and control. Technicians inspect, test, repair, and adjust instruments that detect, measure, and record changes in industrial environments. They work with theoretical or analytical problems, helping engineers improve instrument and system performance.

History

The use of instruments as a means for people to monitor and control their environment and to guide their activities is as old as the sundial. As modern technology progresses, we still find ourselves in need of precise information that is sometimes difficult for a person to physically obtain.

For instance, with the advent of the steam engine in the 19th century, a train operator had to know how much pressure was inside a boiler. A gauge was designed to measure this safely. The early 20th century saw the development of the internal combustion engine and powered flight. With these developments, engineers and technicians designed and made instruments such as speedometers, altimeters, and tachometers to provide vital data for the safe operation of these engines and auxiliary equipment.

Since World War II, instrumentation technology has become a fast-growing field, responding to challenging needs as people explore space, research our oceans, perform biomedical studies, and advance nuclear technology. Today, instrumentation technology involves both measurement and control, and technicians are critical to their accurate operation. For instance, technicians at nuclear reactors assure that the devices inside accurately measure heat, pressure, and radiation, and their rates of change. If any of these factors is not at its specific level, then other instruments make the necessary adjustments. The plant operates safely and efficiently.

The Job

Instrumentation technicians work with complex instruments that detect, measure, and record changes in industrial environments. As part of their duties, these technicians perform tests, develop new instruments, and install, repair, inspect, and maintain the instruments. Examples of such instruments include altimeters, pressure gauges, speedometers, and radiation detection devices.

Some instrumentation technicians operate the laboratory equipment that produces or records the effects of certain conditions on the test instruments, such as vibration, stress, temperature, humidity, pressure, altitude, and acceleration. Other technicians sketch, build, and modify electronic and mechanical fixtures, instruments, and related apparatuses.

As part of their duties, technicians might verify the dimensions and functions of devices assembled by other technicians and craftsworkers, plan test programs, and direct technical personnel in carrying out these tests. Instrumentation technicians also often perform mathematical calculations on instrument readings and test results so they can be used in graphs and written reports.

Instrumentation technicians work with three major categories of instruments: a) *pneumatic and electropneumatic equipment*, which includes temperature and flow transmitters and receivers and devices that start or are started by such things as pressure springs, diaphragms, and bellows; b) *hydraulic instrumentation,* which includes hydraulic valves, hydraulic valve operators, and electrohydraulic equipment; and c) *electrical and electronic equipment,* which includes electrical sensing elements and transducers, electronic recorders, electronic telemetering systems, and electronic computers.

In some industries, a technician might work on equipment from each category, while in other industries, a technician might be responsible for only one specific type of task. The different levels of responsibility depend also on the instrumentation technician's level of training and experience.

Instrumentation technicians may hold a variety of different positions. *Mechanical instrumentation technicians,* for example, handle routine mechanical functions. They check out equipment before operation, calibrate it during operation, rebuild it using standard replacement parts, mount interconnecting equipment from blueprints, and perform routine repairs using common hand tools. They must be able to read both instrumentation and electronic schematic diagrams. *Instrumentation repair technicians* determine the causes of malfunctions and make repairs. Such repairs usually involve individual pieces of equipment, as distinguished from entire systems. This job requires experience, primarily laboratory-oriented, beyond that of mechanical instrumentation technicians.

Troubleshooting instrumentation technicians make adjustments to instruments and control systems, calibrate equipment, set up tests, diagnose malfunctions, and revise existing systems. Their work is performed either on-site or at a workbench. Advanced training in mathematics, physics, and graphics is required for this level of work. Technicians who are involved in the design of instruments are *instrumentation design technicians.* They work under the supervision of a design engineer. Using information prepared by engineers, they build models and prototypes and prepare sketches, working drawings, and diagrams. These technicians also test out new system designs, order parts, and make mock-ups of new systems.

Technicians in certain industries have more specialized duties and responsibilities. *Biomedical equipment technicians* work with instruments used during medical procedures. They receive special training in the biomedical area in which their instruments are used. *Calibration technicians,* also known as *standards laboratory technicians,* work in the electronics industry and in aerospace and aircraft manufacturing. As part of their inspection of systems and instruments, they measure parts for conformity to specifications, and they help develop calibration standards, devise formulas to solve problems in measurement and calibration, and write procedures and practical guides for other calibration technicians.

Electromechanical technicians work with automated mechanical equipment controlled by electronic sensing devices. They assist mechanical engineers in the design and development of such equipment, analyze test results, and write reports. The technician follows blueprints, operates metalworking machines, builds instrument housings, installs electrical equipment, and calibrates instruments and machinery. Technicians who specialize in the assembly of prototype instruments are known as *development technicians*. *Fabrication technicians* specialize in the assembly of production instruments.

Nuclear instrumentation technicians work with instruments at a nuclear power plant. These instruments control the various systems within the nuclear reactor, detect radiation, and sound alarms in case of equipment failure. *Instrument sales technicians* work for equipment manufacturing companies. They analyze customer needs, outline specifications for equipment cost and function, and sometimes do emergency troubleshooting.

Requirements

High School

Math and science courses, such as algebra, geometry, physics, and chemistry, are essential prerequisites to becoming an instrument technician. In addition, machine and electrical shop courses will help you become familiar with electrical, mechanical, and electronic technology. Classes in mechanical drawing and computer-aided drafting are also beneficial. Instrumentation technicians also need good writing and communication skills and should take English, composition, and speech classes.

Postsecondary Training

The basic requirement for an entry-level job is completion of a two-year technical program or equivalent experience in a related field. Such equivalent experience may come from work in an electronics or manufacturing firm or any job that provides experience working with mechanical or electrical equipment.

Technical programs beyond high school can be found in community colleges as well as technical schools. Programs are offered in many different disciplines in addition to instrumentation technology. Programs may be in electronics or in electrical, mechanical, biomedical, or nuclear technology.

Most programs allow technicians to develop hands-on and laboratory skills as well as learn theory. Classes are likely to include instruction on electronic circuitry, computer science, mathematics, and physics. Courses in basic electronics, electrical theory, and graphics are also important. Technical writing is helpful as most technicians will prepare technical reports. Industrial economics, applied psychology, and plant management courses are helpful to those who plan to move into customer service or design.

Certification or Licensing

Instrumentation technicians who graduate from a recognized technical program may become certified by the National Institute for Certification in Engineering Technologies, although this is usually not a required part of a job. Certification is available at various levels, each combining a written exam in one of over 30 specialty fields with a specified amount of job-related experience. Technicians are also eligible to become members of the International Society for Measurement and Control (ISA), which offers an accreditation. Membership in professional organizations is optional but is encouraged as a means of keeping abreast of advancing technology.

Other Requirements

Successful instrumentation technicians need mathematical and scientific aptitudes and the patience to methodically pursue complex questions. A tolerance for following prescribed procedures is essential, especially when undertaking assignments requiring a very precise, unchanging system of problem solving. Successful instrumentation technicians are able to provide solutions quickly and accurately even in stressful situations.

Exploring

As a way to test your abilities and learn more about calibration work, you could build small electronic equipment. Kits for building radios and other small appliances are available in some electronics shops. This gives some basic understanding of electronic components and applications.

Some communities and schools also have clubs for people interested in electronics. They may offer classes that would teach you basic skills in construction, repair, and adjustment of electrical and electronic products. Model building, particularly in hard plastic and steel, will give you a good understanding of how to adapt and fit parts together. It may also help develop hand skills if you want to work with precision instruments.

Visits to industrial laboratories, instrument shops, research laboratories, power installations, and manufacturing companies that rely on automated processes can give you a glimpse at the activities of instrumentation technicians. During such visits, you might be able to speak with technicians about their work or with employers about possible openings in their company. Also, you might look into getting a summer or part-time job as a helper on an industrial maintenance crew.

Employers

Employers of instrumentation technicians include oil refineries, chemical and industrial laboratories, electronics firms, aircraft and aeronautical manufacturers, and biomedical firms. Companies involved in space exploration, oceanographic research, and national defense systems also use technicians. In addition, they work in various capacities in industries, such as the automotive, food, metals, ceramics, pulp and paper, power, textiles, pharmaceuticals, mining, metals, and air and water pollution industries.

Starting Out

Many companies recruit students prior to their graduation. Chemical and medical research companies especially need maintenance and operations technicians and usually recruit at schools where training in these areas is strong. Similarly, many industries in search of design technicians recruit at technical institutes and community colleges where the program is likely to meet their needs.

Students may also get assistance in their job searches through their schools' job placement services, or they may learn about openings through ads in the newspapers. Prospective employees can also apply directly to a company in which they are interested.

Advancement

Entry-level technicians develop their skills by learning tasks on their employers' equipment. Those with good academic records may, upon completion of an employer's basic program, move to an advanced level in sales or another area where a general understanding of the field is more important than specific laboratory skills. Technicians who have developed proficiency in instrumentation may choose to move to a supervisory or specialized position that requires knowledge of a particular aspect of instrumentation.

Earnings

Earnings for instrumentation technicians vary by region. According to the U.S. Bureau of Labor Statistics, the average annual salary of an instrumentation technician is $38,300. Entry-level technicians start at about $20,000, while experienced or specially skilled technicians may earn as much as $64,000 a year. Employee benefits vary but can include paid vacations and holidays, sick leave, insurance benefits, 401-K plans, profit sharing, pension plans, and tuition assistance programs.

Work Environment

Working conditions vary widely for instrumentation technicians. An oil refinery plant job is as different from space mission instrumentation work as a nuclear reactor instrumentation job is different from work in the surgical room of a hospital. All these jobs use similar principles, however, and instrumentation technicians can master new areas by applying what they have learned previously. For technicians who would like to travel, the petroleum industry, in particular, provides employment opportunities in foreign lands.

Instrumentation technicians' tasks may range from the routine to the highly complex and challenging. A calm, well-controlled approach to work is essential. Calibration and adjustment require the dexterity and control of a watchmaker. Consequently, a person who is easily excited or impatient is not well suited to this kind of employment.

Outlook

Employment opportunities for instrumentation technicians will be favorable through 2008. Opportunities will be best for graduates of postsecondary technical training programs. As technology becomes more sophisticated, employers will continue to look for technicians who are skilled in new technology and require a minimum of additional job training.

Most developments in automated manufacturing techniques, including robotics and computer-controlled machinery, rely heavily on instrumentation devices. The emerging fields of air and water pollution control are other areas of growth. Scientists and technicians measure the amount of toxic substances in the air or test water with the use of instrumentation.

Oceanography, including the search for undersea deposits of oil and minerals, is another expanding field for instrumentation technology, as is medical diagnosis, including long-distance diagnosis by physicians through the use of sensors, computers, and telephone lines.

One important field of growth is the teaching profession. As demand rises for skilled technicians, qualified instructors with combined knowledge of theory and application will be needed. Opportunities already exist, not only in educational institutions but also in those industries that have internal training programs.

For More Information

For information on careers and student membership, contact:

International Society for Measurement and Control
PO Box 12277
67 Alexander Drive
Research Triangle Park, NC 27709
Tel: 919-549-8411
Web: http://www.isa.org/

For information on careers and student clubs, contact:

Junior Engineering Technical Society, Inc.
1420 King Street, Suite 405
Alexandria, VA 22314-2794
Tel: 703-548-5387
Web: http://www.jets.org

For information on careers and accreditation, contact:

IEEE Instrumentation and Measurement Society
c/o Institute of Electrical and Electronics Engineers
3 Park Avenue, 17th Floor
New York, NY 10016
Tel: 212-419-7900
Web: http://www.ieee.org/eab/

For information on certification, contact:

National Institute for Certification in Engineering Technologies
1420 King Street
Alexandria, VA 22314-2794
Tel: 888-476-4238
Web: http://www.nicet.org

For information on educational programs and medical instrument certification, contact:

Association for the Advancement of Medical Instrumentation
3330 Washington Boulevard, Suite 400
Arlington, VA 22201-4598
Tel: 800-332-2264
Web: http://www.aami.org

Laser Technicians

School Subjects
Computer science
Mathematics
Physics

Personal Skills
Mechanical/manipulative
Technical/scientific

Work Environment
Primarily indoors
Primarily one location

Minimum Education Level
Associate's degree

Salary Range
$21,000 to $30,000 to $38,000

Certification or Licensing
None available

Outlook
Faster than the average

Overview

Laser technicians produce, install, operate, service, and test laser systems and fiber optics equipment in industrial, medical, or research settings. They work under the direction of engineers or physicists who conduct laboratory activities in laser research and development or design. Depending upon the type of laser system—gas or solid state—a technician generally works either with information systems or with robotics, manufacturing, or medical equipment.

History

The laser was invented in 1958 by the American physicist Gordon Gould. The first working model was a ruby laser, designed and built by Dr. Ted Maiman in 1960. This first working laser created great interest in scientific research laboratories and started intensive experimentation and development in the field of electro-optics.

The word "laser" is actually an acronym, standing for Light Amplification by Stimulated Emission of Radiation. The laser converts electrical power into a special beam of optical or light power. Laser light is different from white light, or light that is produced by ordinary sources. It travels in a parallel beam, diffusing much less than white light. It is also composed of a single color wavelength as opposed to the jumble of colored light waves that make up white light. Because of these unique properties, laser light can be used in a number of different ways.

After its discovery, engineers and scientists considered using the light beam's power in the same ways as electrical power. From 1960 to 1967, various new lasers and electro-optic devices and techniques were developed. Some had considerable optical power, while others had only a small amount of power.

It soon became clear that lasers could be used in a great many ways to solve problems that previously had no practical solution. For example, the concentrated beams of laser light were so powerful that they could drill tiny holes in diamonds, taking minutes where old methods took days.

Lasers began to be used in practical applications, such as surgery, surveying and measuring, industrial product inspection and testing, computers, microprocessors, and manufacturing. As lasers moved from research laboratories to industry, a need arose for workers who were trained in the practical application and technical aspect of the field. In the early 1970s, two-year technical institutes and community colleges began offering specialized training programs in laser technology. The position of laser technician has become a valuable and necessary one in many industries, medical settings, and research programs.

The Job

There are basically two types of laser systems with which laser technicians work: *semiconductor laser systems*, which are the most compact and reliable, and *gas-type lasers*, which are larger and more expensive.

Laser technicians working with semiconductor systems are involved mainly with computer and telephone systems. In addition to helping to test, install, and maintain these systems, technicians work with engineers in their design and improvement.

Technicians who work with gas-type systems usually assist scientists, engineers, or doctors. These systems are used primarily in the fields of robotics, manufacturing, and medical procedures.

Laser technicians perform a wide variety of tasks. Much depends upon their positions and places of employment. For example, some repair lasers and instruct companies on their use, while others work as technicians for very specific applications, such as optical surgery or welding parts.

In general, most technicians are employed in one of five areas: materials processing, communications, military, medical, and research. Technicians are involved in building laser devices in any one of these fields. To build a solid-state laser, they construct, cut, and polish a crystal rod to be used in the laser. They put a flash tube around the crystal and place the unit in a container with a mirror at each end. Using precision instruments, they position the mirrors so that all emitted or reflected light passes through the crystal. Finally, they put the laser body in a chassis, install tubing and wiring to the controls, and place a jacket around the assembly.

There are other duties that all technicians perform, no matter what application they work in. These include taking measurements, cleaning, aligning, inspecting, and operating lasers, and collecting data. Since the laser field is so technologically advanced, computers are used in many tasks and applications. Technicians may be responsible for programming the computers that control the lasers, for inputting data, or for generating reports.

In materials processing, lasers are used for machining, production, measurement, construction, excavation, and photo-optics. Technicians often read and interpret diagrams, schematics, and shop drawings in order to assemble components themselves or oversee the assembly process. They may operate lasers for welding, precision drilling, cutting, and grinding of metal parts, or for trimming and slicing electronic components and circuit elements. They may use lasers to verify precise parts sizes. Finally, technicians may be involved in part marking—using a laser to mark an identifying number or letter on each component. In construction, they may use a laser as a surveying guideline or an aligning tool.

Laser technicians in communications use lasers to generate light impulses transmitted through optical fibers. They help to develop, manufacture, and test optical equipment, and they may design, set up, monitor, and maintain fiber fabrication facilities. This field also uses lasers for data storage and retrieval.

In military and space projects, lasers are frequently used for target-finding, tracking, ranging, identification, and communications. Technicians repair and adapt low-power lasers, which are widely used for these applications.

In medical applications, technicians serve as technical equipment experts and assist physicians and surgeons who use the laser system. They advise on which type of laser and method of delivery to use. They must be on hand during laser procedures to offer recommendations, fine-tune attachments and machines, and troubleshoot should a technical problem occur.

In research and development, lasers are being studied as a source of high-intensity heat in controlled nuclear fusion. These studies are part of the continuing research to produce inexpensive electrical power. Technicians on any research and development team use lasers and electronic devices to perform tests, take measurements, gather data, and make calculations. They may prepare reports for engineers, doctors, scientists, production managers, or lab workers.

Requirements

High School

In high school, a prospective technician can prepare by taking four years of English and at least two years of mathematics, one of which should be algebra. At least one year of physical science, preferably physics, should be included, as well as a class in basic computer programming. Machine shop, basic electronics, and blueprint reading classes are also useful.

Postsecondary Training

Most laser technicians enter the field by attending a two-year program in laser technology at a vocational, technical, or community college. The average associate's degree program in laser technology includes intensive technical and scientific study, with more hours spent in a laboratory or work situation than in the actual classroom. This hands-on experience is supplemented in the first year by courses in mathematics, physics, drafting, diagramming, basic electronics, electronic instrumentation and calibration, introduction to solid-state devices, electromechanical controls, and computer programming.

A second year's study might include courses in geometrical optics, digital circuits, microwaves, laser and electro-optic components, devices and measurements, vacuum techniques, technical report writing, microcomputers, and computer hardware. Special laser projects are often a part of the second year and can help students decide on a specific field. Even after completing their education, technicians typically require further training in the specific practices of their employers.

Other Requirements

Laser technicians are intelligent, with a strong motivation to learn. Technicians have an interest in instruments, laboratory apparatus, and how devices and systems work. Written and spoken communications are very important since technicians often have to work closely with people of varied technological backgrounds.

Physical strength is not usually required, but good manual dexterity and hand-eye and body coordination are quite important. Because lasers can be extremely dangerous, technicians are careful and attentive and willing to follow safety precautions closely. The ability to work efficiently, patiently, and consistently is extremely important for laser technicians, as is a strong ability to solve problems and to do careful, detailed work.

Exploring

Consider your school vocational guidance counselor a valuable resource person. If a community or technical college is nearby, its occupational information center and counseling staff can also be very helpful. In addition, review some of the periodicals that are devoted to the field of lasers. Periodicals such as the *Journal of Laser Applications, Laser Bulletin,* and *Laser Focus World* may offer valuable insight into the field.

Lasers are used in so many places that it should be fairly easy to find a local laser technician, operator, or engineer who can share knowledge about his or her job. It might be possible to find summer or part-time work in construction, manufacturing, or mining where lasers are used in measuring, cutting and welding, and surveying. This type of work can give you a look at jobs in laser technology.

Employers

Laser technicians work in manufacturing, communications, medicine, scientific research, the military, and construction. They can be found in remote areas, by the ocean, in suburbs and in large cities, but most often they are located in cities on the West Coast and in industrial centers of the Northeast.

Starting Out

Colleges that offer associate's degrees in laser technology usually work closely with industry, providing their graduating students with placement services and lists of potential employers. Most laser technicians graduating from a two-year program, in fact, are interviewed and recruited while still in school by representatives of companies that need laser technicians. If hired, they begin working soon after graduation.

Another way to enter the career is to join a branch of the U.S. Armed Forces under a technical training program for laser technicians. Military laser training is not always compatible to civilian training, however, and further study of theory and applications may be needed to enter the field as a civilian.

Advancement

Opportunities for advancement in laser technology are excellent for technicians who keep abreast of advances in the field. In such a relatively new technology, developments occur very rapidly. Workers who investigate and adapt to these changes become more valuable to their employers and advance to greater responsibilities.

Many employers designate various grades or levels for laser technicians, according to experience, education, and job performance. By being promoted through these levels, technicians can advance to supervisory or managerial positions. Supervisors manage a department, supervise other technicians, and train new or current employees.

Mature, experienced, and highly successful laser technicians may decide to become consultants or specialists for individual firms. A consulting position entails working closely with clients, conducting studies and surveys, and proposing improvements, changes, and solutions to problems.

Some technicians move into sales or technical writing positions. Others become instructors in vocational programs, teaching intermediate or advanced laser and fiber optics technology courses.

Earnings

According to a survey done by the Laser Institute of America, the overall average starting salary for laser technicians is between $21,000 and $25,000 per year. Salaries for technicians with at least five years of experience average approximately $30,000 per year, depending on background, experience, and the industry where they are employed.

In addition to salary, technicians usually receive benefits such as insurance, paid holidays and vacations, and retirement plans. Many employers have liberal policies of paying for professional improvement through continued study in school or at work.

Work Environment

Working conditions for laser technicians vary according to the industry. Some spend their day in a laboratory, while others work in a hospital operating room, office, or manufacturing plant. In most cases, however, work areas are kept clean and temperature-controlled in order to protect the laser equipment.

Laser technicians may work at relatively stationary jobs, assembling or operating lasers in the same environment every day, or they may be required to move around frequently, in and out of laboratory areas, production sites, or offices. Some are office- or laboratory-based; others, especially those in sales and service positions, may travel the country.

Laser technicians typically work regular hours. Five eight-hour days per week is the standard, although certain projects may occasionally require overtime.

There are possible hazards in most areas where lasers are used. Because the power supplies for many lasers involve high voltages, technicians frequently work around potentially deadly amounts of electricity. The laser beam itself is also a possible source of serious injury, either through direct exposure to the beam or by reflected light from the laser. Safety precautions, such as wearing protective glasses, are strictly enforced.

Laser technicians handle extremely valuable instruments. The parts used to make lasers are almost always costly. Mistakes that damage lasers or errors in applying lasers can be very costly, running into the thousands of dollars.

Technicians often work as part of a production team or supervisory group, sometimes with scientists and engineers, sometimes as a member of a production team or supervisory group. Some technicians work alone but usually report directly to an engineer, scientist, or manager.

Among the greatest sources of satisfaction for laser technicians is the feeling of success whenever they meet a challenge and see their laser systems perform correctly. This is especially true in sales and service where new users are taught to use this complicated technology and where the technician can actually see customers discovering the effectiveness of lasers. The same satisfaction is felt in research when a new development is proved to be a success.

Outlook

Employment opportunities for laser technicians are expected to be very good through 2008. Rapid changes in technology and continued growth in the industry will almost certainly lead to an increase in the number of technicians employed.

One of the fastest growing areas for laser technicians is fiber optic systems that are used in communications. Optical fiber is replacing wire cables in communication lines and in many electronic products. This trend is expected to continue, so the demand for technicians in the fiber optics field should be especially strong. Growth is also expected to be strong in production, defense, medicine, construction, and entertainment. Technicians interested in research and development, however, should keep in mind that job growth often slows in the face of economic downturns.

For More Information

For information on laser technology and fellowships, contact:

Institute of Electrical and Electronics Engineers
Lasers and Electro-Optical Society
445 Hoes Lane
Piscataway, NJ 08854
Tel: 732-562-3892
Web: http://www.ieee.org/leos

For information on becoming a laser technician, contact:

Laser Institute of America
13501 Ingenuity Drive, Suite 128
Orlando, FL 32826
Tel: 800-345-2737
Web: http://www.laserinstitute.org

Mechanical Engineering Technicians

	School Subjects
English Mathematics Physics	

	Personal Skills
Mechanical/manipulative Technical/scientific	

	Work Environment
Primarily indoors Primarily one location	

	Minimum Education Level
Associate's degree	

	Salary Range
$23,000 to $39,000 to $64,000	

	Certification or Licensing
Voluntary	

	Outlook
About as fast as the average	

Overview

Mechanical engineering technicians work under the direction of mechanical engineers to design, build, maintain, and modify many kinds of machines, mechanical devices, and tools. They work in a wide range of industries and in a variety of specific jobs within every industry.

Mechanical engineering technicians review mechanical drawings and project instructions, analyze design plans to determine costs and practical value, sketch rough layouts of proposed machines or parts, assemble new or modified devices or components, test completed assemblies or components, analyze test results, and write reports.

History

Mechanical engineering dates back to ancient times, when it was used almost exclusively for military purposes. Perhaps the Romans were the first to use the science for nonmilitary projects, such as aqueducts, roads, and bridges, although many if not most of these structures were built to advance military objectives.

With the advent of the Industrial Revolution and the use of machines for manufacturing, mechanical engineering technology took a giant step forward. One of the most important figures in this revolution was Eli Whitney. Having received a government contract in 1798 to produce 15,000 muskets, he hired not gunsmiths, but mechanics. At that time, all articles, including muskets, were built one by one by individual craft workers. No two muskets were ever alike.

Whitney took a different approach. For two years after receiving the contract, he focused on developing and building special-purpose machines, and then trained mechanics to make specific parts of the gun. When he was finished, Whitney had invented new machine tools and attachments, such as the milling machine and jig; made real the concept of interchangeable parts; and paved the way for the modern manufacturing assembly line.

This manufacturing process required not only ingenious inventors and skilled mechanics to operate the machines, but also skilled assistants to help develop new machines, set or reset tolerances, maintain and repair operational equipment, and direct, supervise, and instruct workers. These assistants are today's mechanical engineering technicians, a crucial part of today's engineering team. In addition to manufacturing, they are employed in almost every application that uses mechanical principles.

The Job

Mechanical engineering technicians are employed in a broad range of industries. Technicians may specialize in any one of many areas including biomedical equipment, measurement and control, products manufacturing, solar energy, turbo machinery, energy resource technology, and engineering materials and technology.

Within each application, there are various aspects of the work with which the technician may be involved. One phase is research and development. In this area, the mechanical technician may assist an engineer or scientist in the design and development of anything from a ballpoint to a sophisticated measuring device. These technicians prepare rough sketches and layouts of the project being developed.

In the design of an automobile engine, for example, engineering technicians make drawings that detail the fans, pistons, connecting rods, and flywheels to be used in the engine. They estimate cost and operational qualities of each part, taking into account friction, stress, strain, and vibration. By performing these tasks, they free the engineer to accomplish other research assignments.

A second common type of work for mechanical engineering technicians is testing. For products such as engines, motors, or other moving devices, technicians may set up prototypes of the equipment to be tested and run performance tests. Some tests require one procedure to be done repeatedly, while others require that equipment be run over long periods of time to observe any changes in operation. Technicians collect and compile all necessary data from the testing procedures and prepare reports for the engineer or scientist.

In the manufacture of a product, preparations must be made for its production. In this effort, mechanical engineering technicians assist in the product design by making final design layouts and detailed drawings of parts to be manufactured and of any special manufacturing equipment needed. Some test and inspect machines and equipment or work with engineers to eliminate production problems.

Other mechanical engineering technicians examine plans and drawings to determine what materials are needed and prepare lists of these materials, specifying quality, size, and strength. They also may estimate labor costs, equipment life, and plant space needed. After the product is manufactured, some mechanical engineering technicians may help solve storage and shipping problems, while others assist in customer relations when product installation is required.

Some engineering technicians work with tool designers. They help in preparing sketches of designs for cutting tools, jigs, special fixtures, and other devices used in mass production. Frequently, they redesign existing tools to improve their efficiency.

Requirements

High School

Preparation for this career begins in high school. Although entrance requirements to associate programs vary somewhat from school to school, mathematics and physical science form the backbone of a good preparatory curriculum. Classes should include algebra, geometry, science, computer science, mechanical drawing, shop, and communications.

Postsecondary Training

Associate's degree or two-year mechanical technician programs are designed to prepare students for entry-level positions. Most programs accredited by the Accreditation Board for Engineering and Technology (ABET) offer one year of a basic program with a chance to specialize in the second year. The first year of the program generally consists of courses in college algebra and trigonometry, science, and communications skills. Other classes introduce students to the manufacturing processes, drafting, and language of the industry.

The second year's courses focus on mechanical technology. These include fluid mechanics, thermodynamics, tool and machine design, instruments and controls, production technology, electricity, and electronics. Many schools allow their students to choose a major in the second year of the program, which provides training for a specific area of work in the manufacturing industry.

Certification or Licensing

Many mechanical engineering technicians choose to become certified by the National Institute for Certification in Engineering Technologies (NICET). To become certified, a technician must combine a specific amount of job-related experience with a written examination. Certifications are offered at several levels of expertise. Such certification is generally voluntary, although obtaining certification shows a high level of commitment and dedication that employers find highly desirable.

Mechanical engineering technicians are encouraged to become affiliated with professional groups, such as the American Society of Certified Engineering Technicians, that offer continuing education sessions for members. Some mechanical engineering technicians may be required to belong to unions.

Other Requirements

Technicians need mathematical and mechanical aptitude. They understand abstract concepts and apply scientific principles to problems in the shop or laboratory, in both the design and the manufacturing process. They are interested in people and machines and have the ability to carry out detailed work. They analyze sketches and drawings and possess patience, perseverance, and resourcefulness. Additionally, they have good communication skills and can present both spoken and written reports.

Exploring

You may be able to obtain part-time or summer work in a machine shop or factory. This type of work usually consists of sweeping floors and clearing out machine tools, but it offers an opportunity to view the field firsthand and also demonstrates interest to future employers. Field trips to industrial laboratories, drafting studios, or manufacturing facilities can offer overall views of this type of work. Hobbies like automobile repair, model making, and electronic kit assembling can also be helpful. Finally, any high school student interested in the engineering field should consider joining the Junior Engineering Technical Society (JETS).

Employers

Many engineering technicians work in durable goods manufacturing, primarily making electrical and electronic machinery and equipment, industrial machinery and equipment, instruments and related products, and transportation equipment. A sizable percentage work is in service industries, mostly in engineering and business services companies that do contract work for government, manufacturing, and other organizations.

The federal government employs engineering technicians in the Departments of Defense, Transportation, Agriculture, and Interior as well as the Tennessee Valley Authority and the National Aeronautics and Space

Administration. State and municipal governments also have engineering technicians working for them.

Starting Out

Schools offering associate's degrees in mechanical engineering technology and two-year technician programs usually help graduates find employment. At most colleges, in fact, company recruiters interview prospective graduates during their final semester of school. As a result, many students receive job offers before graduation. Other graduates may prefer to apply directly to employers, use newspaper classified ads, or apply through public or private employment services.

Advancement

As mechanical engineering technicians remain with a company, they become more valuable to the employer. Opportunities for advancement are available to those who are willing to accept greater responsibilities either by specializing in a specific field, taking on more technically complex assignments, or by assuming supervisory duties. Some technicians advance by moving into technical sales or customer relations. Mechanical technicians who further their education may choose to become tool designers or mechanical engineers.

Earnings

Salaries for mechanical engineering technicians vary depending on the nature and location of the job, employer, amount of training the technician has received, and number of years of experience.

In general, mechanical engineering technicians who develop and test machinery and equipment under the direction of an engineering staff earn between $28,000 and $50,000 a year. The average in 1997 was about $39,000, according to the U.S. Bureau of Labor Statistics. Some mechanical engineering technicians, especially those at the beginning of their careers, may make around $23,000 a year or less, while some senior technicians with special skills and experience may make from $50,000 to $64,000 a year or more.

These salaries are based upon the standard workweek. Overtime or premium time pay may be earned for work beyond regular daytime hours or workweek. Other benefits, depending on the company and union agreements, include paid vacation days, insurance, retirement plans, profit sharing, and tuition-reimbursement plans.

Work Environment

Mechanical engineering technicians work in a variety of conditions, depending on their field of specialization. Technicians who specialize in design may find that they spend most of their time at the drafting board or computer. Those who specialize in manufacturing may spend some time at a desk, but also spend considerable time in manufacturing areas or shops.

Conditions also vary according to industry. Some industries require technicians to work in foundries, die-casting rooms, machine shops, assembly areas, or punch-press areas. Most of these areas, however, are well lighted, heated, and ventilated. Moreover, most industries employing mechanical engineering technicians have strong safety programs.

Mechanical engineering technicians are often called upon to exercise decision-making skills, to be responsible for valuable equipment, and to act as effective leaders. At other times they carry out routine, uncomplicated tasks. Similarly, in some cases, they may coordinate the activities of others, while at other times, they are the ones supervised. They must be able to respond well to both types of demands. In return for this flexibility and versatility, mechanical engineering technicians are usually highly respected by their employers and coworkers.

Outlook

Job opportunities for mechanical engineering technicians are expected to grow as quickly as the average through 2008. Manufacturing companies will be looking for more ways to apply the advances in mechanical technology to their operations. Opportunities will be best for technicians who are skilled in new manufacturing concepts, materials, and designs. Many job openings also will be created by people retiring or leaving the field.

However, the employment outlook for engineering technicians is influenced by the economy. Hiring will fluctuate with the ups and downs of the nation's overall economic situation. Technicians whose jobs are defense-related may experience fewer opportunities because of recent defense cutbacks.

For More Information

For information on colleges and universities offering accredited programs in engineering technology, contact:

Accreditation Board for Engineering and Technology, Inc.
111 Market Place, Suite 1050
Baltimore, MD 21202
Tel: 410-347-7700
Web: http://www.abet.org

For information about membership in a professional society for engineering technicians, contact:

American Society of Certified Engineering Technicians
PO Box 1348
Flowery Branch, GA 30542
Tel: 770-967-9173

For information about the field of mechanical engineering, contact:

American Society of Mechanical Engineers
3 Park Avenue
New York, NY 10016-5990
Tel: 212-591-7000
Web: http://www.asme.org

For information on high school programs that provide opportunities to learn about engineering technology, contact:

Junior Engineering Technical Society, Inc.
1420 King Street, Suite 405
Alexandria, VA 22314-2794
Tel: 703-548-5387
Web: http://www.jets.org

For information on certification of mechanical engineering technicians, contact:

National Institute for Certification in Engineering Technologies
1420 King Street
Alexandria, VA 22314-2715
Tel: 888-476-4238
Web: http://www.nicet.org

Microelectronics Technicians

School Subjects
English
Mathematics
Physics

Personal Skills
Mechanical/manipulative
Technical/scientific

Work Environment
Primarily indoors
Primarily one location

Minimum Education Level
Associate's degree

Salary Range
$28,000 to $33,000 to $50,000+

Certification or Licensing
Voluntary

Outlook
Faster than the average

Overview

Microelectronics technicians work in research laboratories assisting the engineering staff to develop and construct prototype and custom-designed microchips. Microchips, often called simply "chips," are tiny but extremely complex electronic devices, which control the operations of many kinds of communications equipment, consumer products, industrial controls, aerospace guidance systems, and medical electronics. The process of manufacturing chips is often called fabrication. About 335,000 people work as electrical and electronics engineering technicians.

History

The science of electronics is only about 100 years old. Yet electronics has had an enormous impact on the way people live. Without electronics, things like television, computers, X-ray machines, and radar would not be possible. Today, nearly every area of industry, manufacturing, entertainment, health care, and communications uses electronics to improve the quality of people's lives. This article you are reading, for example, was created by people using electronic equipment, from the writing of each article to the design, layout, and production of the book itself.

The earliest electronic systems depended on electron vacuum tubes to conduct current. But these devices were too bulky and too slow for many of their desired tasks. In the early 1950s, the introduction of microelectronics—that is, the design and production of integrated circuits and products using integrated circuits—allowed engineers and scientists to design faster and faster and smaller and smaller electronic devices. Initially developed for military equipment and space technology, integrated circuits have made possible such everyday products as personal computers, microwave ovens, and videocassette recorders and are found in nearly every electronic product that people use today.

Integrated circuits are miniaturized electronic systems. Integrated circuits include many interconnected electronic components such as transistors, capacitors, and resistors, produced on or in a single thin slice of a semiconductor material. Semiconductors are so named because they are substances with electrical properties somewhere between those of conductors and insulators. The semiconductor used most frequently in microchips is silicon, so microchips are also sometimes called silicon chips. Often smaller than a fingernail, chips may contain multiple layers of complex circuitry stacked on top of each other. The word "integrated" refers to the way the circuitry is blended into the chip during the fabrication process.

The reliance on electronic technology has created a need for skilled personnel to design, construct, test, and repair electronic components and products. The growing uses of microelectronics has created a corresponding demand for technicians specially trained to assist in the design and development of new applications of electronic technology.

The Job

Microelectronics technicians typically assist in the development of proto-types, or new kinds, of electronic components and products. They work closely with *electronics engineers*, who design the components, build and test them, and prepare the component or product for large-scale manufacture. Such components usually require the integrated operation of several or many different types of chips.

Microelectronics technicians generally work from a schematic received from the design engineer. The schematic contains a list of the parts that will be needed to construct the component and the layout that the technician will follow. The technician will gather the parts and prepare the materials to be used. Following the schematic, the technician constructs the component and then uses a variety of sophisticated, highly sensitive equipment to test the component's performance. One such test measures the component's "burn-in time." During this test the component is kept in continuous operation for a long period of time, and the component and its various features are subject-ed to a variety of tests to be certain the component will stand up to extend-ed use.

If the component fails to function according to its required specifica-tions, the microelectronics technician must be able to troubleshoot the design, locating where the component has failed, and replace one part for a new or different part. Test results are reported to the engineering staff, and the technician may be required to help in evaluating the results and prepar-ing reports based on these evaluations. In many situations, the microelec-tronics technician will work closely with the engineer to solve any problems arising in the component's operation and design.

After the testing period, the microelectronics technician is often respon-sible for assisting in the technical writing of the component's specifications. These specifications are used for integrating the component into new or redesigned products or for developing the process for the component's large-scale manufacture. The microelectronics technician helps to develop the pro-duction system for the component and will also write reports on the com-ponent's functions, uses, and performance.

"You really need to have good communication skills," says Kyle Turner, a microelectronics technician at White Oak Semi-Conductor in Sandstone, Virginia. "Not only do you have to let others know what you mean and explain yourself, you often have to train new employees in the specifics of our product."

Microelectronics technicians perform many of the same functions of electronics technicians, but generally work only in the development labora-tory. More experienced technicians may assume greater responsibilities. They work closely with the engineering staff to develop layout and assembly procedures and to use their own knowledge of microelectronics to suggest changes in circuitry or installation. Often they are depended upon to simplify the assembly or maintenance requirements. After making any changes, they will test the performance of the component, analyze the results, and suggest and perform further modifications to the component's design. Technicians may fabricate new parts using various machine tools, supervise the installation of the new component, or become involved in training and supervising other technical personnel.

Some microelectronics technicians specialize in the fabrication and testing of semiconductors and integrated circuits. These technicians are usually called *semiconductor development technicians*. They are involved in the development of prototype chips, following the direction of engineering staff, and perform the various steps required for making and testing new integrated circuits.

Requirements

The advanced technology involved in microelectronics means that post-high school education or training is a requirement for entering the field. Students should consider enrolling in two-year training programs at a community college or vocational training facility and expect to earn a certificate or an associate's degree. Like most microelectronics technicians, Turner completed a two-year degree in electronics as well as an extensive on-the-job training program.

High School

High school students interested in microelectronics can begin their preparation by taking courses such as algebra and geometry. Students who have taken science courses, especially chemistry and physics, will have a better chance to enter an apprenticeship program and will be more prepared for postsecondary educational programs.

"Math skills are really important," says Turner. "You have to be able to take accurate measurements and make good calculations."

Knowledge of proper grammar and spelling is necessary for writing reports, and students should also develop their reading comprehension. Taking industrial classes, such as metalworking, wood shop, auto shop, and machine shop, and similar courses in plastics, electronics, and construction techniques will be helpful. Another area of study for the prospective microelectronics technician is computer science, and students would do well to seek experience in computer technology.

Postsecondary Training

Few employers will hire people for microelectronics technician positions who do not have advanced training. Although some low-skilled workers may advance into technician jobs, employers generally prefer to hire people with higher education. Technician and associate's degree programs are available at many community colleges and at public and private vocational training centers and schools. Many technical schools are located where the microelectronics industry is particularly active. These schools often have programs tailored specifically for the needs of companies in their area. Community colleges offer a greater degree of flexibility in that they are able to keep up with the rapid advances and changes in technology and can redesign their courses and programs to meet the new requirements. Students can expect to study in such areas as mathematics, including algebra, geometry, and calculus; physics; and electronic engineering technology. Many schools will require students to take courses in English composition, as well as fulfill other course requirements in the humanities and social sciences.

Other methods of entry are three- and four-year apprenticeship programs. These programs generally involve on-the-job training by the employer. Students can locate apprenticeship opportunities through their high school guidance office, in listings in local newspapers, or by contacting local manufacturers.

Military service is also an excellent method for beginning an electronics career. The military is one of the largest users of electronics technology and offers training and educational programs to enlisted personnel in many areas of electronics.

Finally, the rapid advancements in microelectronics may make it desirable or even necessary for the microelectronics technician to continue to take courses, receive training, and study various trade journals throughout his or her career.

Certification or Licensing

Certification is not mandatory in most areas of electronics (although technicians working with radio-transmitting devices are required to be licensed by the Federal Communications Commission), but voluntary certification may prove useful in locating work and in increasing your pay and responsibilities.

The International Society of Certified Electronics Technicians (ISCET) offers certification testing to technicians with four years of experience or schooling, as well as associate-level testing of basic electronics for beginning technicians. ISCET also offers a variety of study and training materials to help prepare for the certification tests.

Other Requirements

Microelectronics technicians are involved in creating prototypes—that is, new and untested technology. This aspect of the field brings special responsibilities for carrying out assembly and testing procedures: these must be performed with a high degree of precision. When assembling a new component, for example, the microelectronics technician must be able to follow the design engineer's specifications and instructions exactly. Similar diligence and attention to detail are necessary when following the different procedures for testing the new components. An understanding of the underlying technology is important.

Exploring

You can begin exploring this field by getting involved in science clubs and working on electronics projects at home. Any part-time experience repairing electronic equipment will give you exposure to the basics of electronics.

You can find many resources for electronics experiments and projects in your school or local library or on the Internet. Summer employment in any type of electronics will be useful. Talking with someone who works in the field may help you narrow your focus to one particular area of electronics.

Employers

About 406,000 people worked as electronics and electrical service technicians in the late 1990s. Many of these technicians work in the computers, electronics, and communications fields. Because these fields are geographically concentrated in California, Texas, and Massachusetts, many electronics technician jobs are located in these areas. There are positions available elsewhere, but many technicians relocate to work in these concentrated areas.

Some electronics technicians are self-employed, some work for large corporations, and others work in government-related jobs.

Starting Out

Most schools provide job placement services to students completing their degree program. Many offer on-the-job training as a part of the program. An internship or other "real-life" experience is desirable but not necessary. Many companies have extensive on-site training programs.

Newspapers and trade journals are full of openings for people working in electronics, and some companies recruit new hires directly on campus. Government employment offices are also good sources when looking for job leads.

Advancement

Microelectronics technicians who choose to continue their education can expect to increase their responsibilities and be eligible to advance to supervisory and managerial positions.

Microelectronics technicians may also desire to enter other, more demanding areas of microelectronics, such as semiconductor development and engineering. Additional education may be necessary; engineers will be required to hold at least a four-year degree in electronic engineering.

Becoming a Certified Electronics Technician with testing from the International Society of Certified Electronics Technicians may be part of the requirement for advancement in certain companies.

Earnings

Microelectronics technicians earn an average starting salary of $28,000, according to the U.S. Department of Labor. Those in managerial or supervisory positions earn higher salaries, ranging between $33,000 and $50,000 per year. Wage rates vary greatly, according to skill-level, type of employer, and location. Most employers offer some fringe benefits, including paid holidays and vacations, sick leave, and life and health insurance.

Work Environment

Microelectronics technicians generally work a 40-hour week, although they may be assigned to different shifts or be required to work weekends and holidays. Overtime and holiday pay can usually be expected in such circumstances. The work setting is extremely clean, well lighted, and dust free.

The variety of a microelectronics technician's duties requires flexibility on the job. All the different tasks involved in the job requires that the microelectronics technician wear many hats. They have to be exact no matter what they're doing, whether building an electronic component, running the tests, or recording the data. The fact that each day is often very different from the one before it is an aspect of the job that many technicians find appealing.

"One of the best things about the job is that it's always changing. We're always trying to make a better product, reduce cycle time, make it smaller or cheaper," says Turner. "You're always learning because it changes like crazy."

Outlook

Jobs in the electronics industry are expected to grow faster than the average through 2008, according to the U.S. Department of Labor. This is because of increasing competition within the industry and the rapid technological advances that characterize the electronics industry. Electronics is also a rapidly growing industry, and the use of electronic technology will become more and more important to every aspect of people's lives. This in turn will create a demand for workers with the skills and training to sustain the industry's growth. In addition, as more and more manufacturers adapt electronic technology to their products and manufacturing processes, the need for skilled personnel will also increase.

The increasing reliability and durability of electronics technology, however, will have some effect on the need for technicians. Similarly, increasing imports of microelectronics products, components, and technology may represent a decrease in production in this country, which will in turn decrease the numbers of microelectronics technicians needed here. Nevertheless, the government will continue to account for a large part of the demand for microelectronics components, technology, and personnel.

For More Information

For information on certification, contact:

International Society of Certified Electronics Technicians
2708 West Berry Street
Fort Worth, TX 76109-2356
Tel: 817-921-9101
Email: iscetFW@aol.com
Web: http://www.iscet.org/

Optics Technicians

School Subjects	Biology Chemistry
Personal Skills	Helping/teaching Technical/scientific
Work Environment	Primarily indoors Primarily one location
Minimum Education Level	Some postsecondary training
Salary Range	$15,000 to $31,500 to $54,000+
Certification or Licensing	Required in some fields
Outlook	Little change or more slowly than the average

Overview

Optics technicians design, fabricate, assemble, or install optical instruments, such as telescopes, microscopes, aerial cameras, and eyeglasses. The four most common types of optics technicians are optomechanical technicians, precision-lens technicians, precision-lens grinders (sometimes called *optical technicians*), and photo-optics technicians.

In general, these four careers may be distinguished from one another in the following ways: *Optomechanical technicians* build and test complete optical and optomechanical devices. *Precision-lens technicians* handle the whole range of manufacturing activities to fabricate the lenses that go into optical and optomechanical devices. *Precision-lens grinders* grind, polish, cement, and inspect the lens. *Photo-optics technicians* install, maintain, or actually use the optical or optomechanical devices for scientific and engineering measurements and projects.

History

Humans have been using simple lenses for magnification for more than 1,000 years, and eyeglasses have been in use since the 14th century. More complex optical instruments, however, such as the microscope and telescope, were not developed until the 17th century. These first microscopes and telescopes were crude by modern standards, as the first lenses of moderately good quality for these instruments were not developed until the 19th century.

During the 19th century, many of the basic principles used for making the calculations necessary for lens design were expounded, first in a book by Karl Friedrich Gauss (1777-1885) published in 1841 and later in other studies based on Gauss's work during the 1850s. These principles remained the basis for making the calculations needed for lens design until around 1960, when computer modeling became the predominant way to design lenses.

Up until the early part of the 20th century, engineering problems associated with the design of optical instruments were handled by mechanical engineers, physicists, and mathematicians. During World War I, however, because of the increasingly important applications of optical instruments, optical engineering emerged as a separate discipline, and today it is taught in a separate department in many universities.

And, in the same way, the optics technicians described in this article emerged as distinct from all other engineering and science technicians. They have their own instructional programs, their own professional societies, and their own licensing procedures.

The Job

The optical manufacturing industry offers many different types of jobs for the skilled and well-trained technician. There are jobs, especially for optomechanical technicians, that mostly involve scientific and theoretical matters. There are other jobs, such as those that precision-lens grinders often perform, that focus on craft-working skills. The work of precision-lens technicians, most of all but for many other optics technicians as well, combines both of these kinds of activities. Finally, there are many jobs for optics technicians, but especially for photo-optics technicians, that require the mechanical skills and ingenuity of a repairer and troubleshooter.

In general, optics technicians are employed in one of the following areas: research and development, product manufacture, maintenance and operations, and lens fabrication.

Technicians working in the research and development area seek to create new optical instruments or new applications for existing instruments. They are often called upon to invent new techniques to conduct experiments, obtain measurements, or carry out fabrication procedures requested by engineers or scientists.

Among the products that research-and-development technicians may be involved with are night-vision instruments for surveillance and security, ultraprecise distance-measuring devices, and instruments for analysis of medical and clinical specimens, monitoring patients, and routine inspection of materials including industrial wastes.

Technicians in the product-manufacturing area work mostly at the assembly, alignment, calibration, and testing of common optical instruments, such as microscopes, telescopes, binoculars, and cameras. They may also help produce less common devices, such as transits and levels for surveying or spectrographs and spectrophotometers used in medical research and diagnosis.

A relatively new field that allows both research-and-development technicians and product-development technicians opportunities to combine their interests in optics and photography is the development and production of integrated electronic circuits. These highly complex, tiny devices are widely used in calculators, computers, television equipment, and control devices for electronic systems, whether in the cockpit of a jet airliner or in the control room of an electric generating plant. The manufacture of these electronic circuits requires a wide variety of skills, from the production of large patterns and plans, called art work, to the alignment and operation of the microcameras that produce the extraordinarily small printing negatives used to make the final circuits on the tiny metallic chips that are the basis of the integrated circuits.

In the field of maintenance and operations, technicians are involved with the on-site use of optical instruments, such as technical and scientific cameras, large observatory telescopes and auxiliary instruments, light-measuring equipment, and spectrophotometers, some of which operate with invisible or ultraviolet radiation.

Operations and maintenance technicians (usually photo-optics technicians) may find themselves working at a rocket or missile test range or at a missile or satellite tracking station, where they may be assembling, adjusting, aligning, or operating telescopic cameras that produce some of the most important information about missiles in flight. These cameras are often as big as the telescopes used by astronomers, and they weigh up to 15 tons. Large powerful motors enable the camera to rotate and, thus, to follow a rocket in flight until it comes down. The picture information gathered by these long-range tracking cameras is often the only clue to missile flight errors or failure, as there is often virtually nothing left of a missile after it lands.

Another kind of optics technician, called a *photonics technician*, works in a specialized area of optics called photonics. Photonics is a technology that uses photons, or particles of light, to process information. It includes lasers, fiber optics, optical instruments, and related electronics. Photonics technicians assist engineers in developing applications utilizing photonics. One such application is a wireless data communications network that links computer workstations through infrared technology. Photonics is being used in areas such as data communications, including using photons to send information through optical cables for telephone and computer communications, solar energy products, holograms, and compact discs.

In the lens-fabrication area there are many different kinds of jobs for optics technicians. *Lens molders* work with partially melted glass. Their principal task usually is to press the partially melted glass into rough lens blanks. *Lens blockers* assist senior lens makers in setting lens blanks into holders in preparation for curve generating, grinding, and polishing. *Lens generators*, using special grinding machines, give the glass blanks the correct curvature as they are held in the holders. *Lens grinders* work with cup-shaped tools and fine grinding powders. They bring the blanks in the holders to the required curve within close tolerances. *Lens polishers* use ultrafine powders and special tools made of pitch or beeswax to bring the surfaces of the fine-ground blank to bright, clear polish. *Lens centerers* or *lens edgers* make true, or perfect, the various optical elements with finished spherical surfaces. *Optical-coating technicians* carefully clean finished lenses and install them inside a vacuum chamber. Special mineral materials are then boiled in small, electrically heated vessels in the vacuum, and the vapor condenses on the lenses to form extremely thin layers that reduce glass surface reflections. *Quality inspectors* examine the finished lenses for tiny scratches, discolorations of the coating, and other faults or errors that may require rejection of the finished element before it is assembled into an instrument.

Requirements

High School

If you are considering a career as an optics technician, you should take courses that provide a strong general background and prepare you for further study in technical fields, including mathematics, science, technical reading and writing, and shop. Courses in photography, particularly those involving darkroom work, are also valuable, since photography plays an important role in many fields where optics technicians work.

Postsecondary Training

There are only a few schools that offer specific training for optics technicians. A good alternate way to obtain advanced education is to attend a technical institute or community college where two- or three-year engineering or science programs are available and to pick out those courses best suited for a career as an optics technician.

During the first year of a two-year program, students should take courses in geometrical optics, trigonometry, lens polishing, technical writing, optical instruments, analytical geometry, and specifications writing. During the second year, the student may take courses in physics, optical shop practices, manual preparation, mechanical drawing, and report preparation.

Prospective optics technicians should be aware that some large corporations have training programs for beginning technicians. These programs are not always publicized and may take some searching to find. There are also some commercially run technical schools that provide training; however, they are often costly and should be investigated carefully, preferably by talking to former students, before undertaking such a program.

Certification or Licensing

Except for those optics technicians who make and dispense eyeglasses, there are no licensing requirements. However, in some areas of optics technology, it is necessary to know government requirements for safety and to obtain safety certificates. In a few cases, the correct function of an instrument to be used in a government application or for medical or clinical purposes must be legally certified by the technician. In these instances, technicians should discuss the certification requirements with their employer or supervisor.

Other Requirements

Optics technicians should have a strong interest in and a good aptitude for mathematics and physics. Patience, care, and good manual skills are important to design precision telescopic lenses, grind and polish the glass elements, and assemble and align the instrument.

Exploring

One of the best ways for students to gain experience in and exposure to the field of optics is through membership in a club or organization related to this field. These include hobby clubs, student societies, or groups with scientific interests. Some examples include the following: organizations for amateur astronomers, amateur radio builders and operators, and amateur telescope makers; and school clubs in photography, especially those involving activities with film processing, print and enlargement making, and camera operations.

Through visits to industrial laboratories or manufacturing companies, you can witness technicians actually involved in their work and may be able to speak with several of these people regarding their work or with employers about possibilities for technicians in that particular industry or company.

Employers

Optical grinding and polishing shops provide employment opportunities. One of the largest employers of optical technicians are the space programs and weapons-development programs run by the military. Other employment opportunities are available with manufacturers of optical instruments, such as microscopes, telescopes, binoculars, cameras, and advanced medical equipment.

Starting Out

Many students enrolled in two-year training programs can find jobs through interviews with company recruiters conducted on campus during the second year of their program. Other students find employment through participating in work-study programs while enrolled in school. In many cases, the student's part-time employer will offer full-time work after graduation or provide leads on other possible jobs.

For students who do not find suitable employment in one of these ways, there are some employment agencies that specialize in placing personnel in the optics industry. There are also very active societies in the optical, photographic, physical science, and engineering fields that can be sources of worthwhile job leads. Contact technical societies for advice and help in job hunting. The primary purpose of a technical society is to aid the industry it represents, and there is no better way the society can do this than to attract interested people into the field and help them find their best job.

Advancement

As technicians gain experience and additional skills, new and more demanding jobs are offered to them. The following paragraphs describe some of the jobs to which experienced technicians may advance.

Hand lens figurers shape some lenses and optical elements, using hand-operated grinding and polishing methods. These shapes are called "aspheric," as they cannot be made by the normal mass-production grinding and generating machines. Special highly sensitive test machines are used to aid these advanced polishing technicians.

Photographic technicians use the camera in many important research and engineering projects, as well as in the production of optical items such as reticles (cross hairs or wires in the focus of the eyepiece of an optical instrument), optical test targets, and integrated electronic circuits. These technicians will be involved in the operation of cameras and with photographic laboratory work, sometimes leading a team of technicians in these tasks.

Instrument assemblers and testers direct the assembly of various parts into the final instrument, performing certain critical assembly tasks themselves. When the instrument is complete, they, or other technicians under their direction, check the instrument's alignment, functioning, appearance, and readiness for the customer.

Optical model makers work with specially made or purchased components to assemble a prototype or first model of a new instrument under the direction of the engineer in charge. These technicians must be able to keep the prototype in operation, so that the engineer may develop knowledge and understanding of production problems.

Research and development technicians help to make and assemble new instruments and apparatus in close cooperation with scientists and engineers. The opportunities for self-expression and innovation are highest in this area.

Earnings

Salaries and wages vary according to the industry and the type of work the technician is doing. In general, starting salaries for technicians who have completed a two-year postsecondary training program range from around $15,724 to $24,086 a year. Technicians involved in apprenticeship training may receive reduced wages during the early stages of their apprenticeships. Technicians who have not completed a two-year training program receive starting salaries several hundred dollars a year less than technicians in the same industry who have completed such a program.

Most technicians who are graduates of these programs and who have advanced beyond the entry level earn salaries that range from $21,000 to $31,500 a year and average around $26,300 a year. Senior technicians receive average salaries ranging from $33,000 to $54,000 a year, or more, depending on their employers and type of work performed.

Work Environment

In some polishing and hand-figuring rooms, and in the first assembly rooms, it is sometimes necessary to provide special dust, humidity, and temperature controls. The technicians are required to wear clean, lint-free garments, and to use caps and overshoe covers. These rooms are widely used whenever the work requires the most meticulous cleanliness, since a single piece of lint might cause the loss of an entire component or assembly.

On the other hand, technicians working with large astronomical telescopes, with missile-tracking cameras on a military test range, or with instrument cameras for recording outdoor activities will have to work in a variety of conditions.

Very often, optics technicians, particularly those associated with the assembly, alignment, and testing of complete instruments, will find themselves working in the dark or at night. In very few cases is the work apt to be grimy or dangerous.

Part of the discipline of optics is concentrated in the scientific and technical world, another in the world of the skilled artisan working with the hands and eyes. For prospective optics technicians who have an interest in and an aptitude for both of these kinds of activities, optics technology provides many opportunities to make personal contributions to the advancement and development of optical science and the optical industry.

Because optics technology is involved in creating the instruments and equipment necessary in ever-expanding fields such as medical research, space exploration, communications systems, and microcircuitry design and manufacture, optics technicians can feel some satisfaction in knowing that they are working in some of today's most exciting fields of scientific and technological research. The work that optics technicians perform directly affects the lives of most Americans.

As with all technicians in the engineering and science field, optics technicians are often called upon to perform both very challenging and very routine and repetitive work. Optics technology offers technicians a spectrum of jobs, so that prospective technicians can choose those that fit their temperaments. However, almost all technicians should expect some mixture of the routine and the challenging in their jobs.

Optics technicians almost always work as part of a group effort. Often they serve as intermediaries between scientists and engineers who run projects and skilled craftsworkers who carry out much of the work.

Outlook

The field of optics technology and manufacturing should have little growth through 2008. Traditionally, the space program and weapons-development programs run by the military have been employers of large numbers of optics technicians. Employment in this field is determined by levels of government spending and is difficult to predict. Even if there are cutbacks in this spending, however, the public demand for modern complex cameras, binoculars, and telescopes and the need for advanced medical equipment should sustain employment levels for most kinds of optics technicians.

For More Information

For information on optics and career opportunities, contact these organizations:

American Precision Optics Manufacturers Association
University of Rochester
PO Box 20001
Rochester, NY 14602
Email: info@apomanet.org
Web: http://www.apomanet.org/

Junior Engineering Technical Society, Inc.
1420 King Street, Suite 405
Alexandria, VA 22314-2794
Tel: 703-548-5387
Email: jets@nas.edu
Web: http://www.jets.org

For information on student membership, contact:

Optical Society of America
2010 Massachusetts Avenue, NW
Washington, DC 20036
Tel: 202-223-8130
Web: http://www.osa.org

For information on careers and educational programs, contact SPIE:

SPIE—The International Society for Optical Engineering
PO Box 10
1000 20th Street
Bellingham, WA 98227-0010
Tel: 360-676-3290
Web: http://www.spie.org/

Packaging Machinery Technicians

	School Subjects
Mathematics	
Technical/Shop	

	Personal Skills
Mechanical/manipulative	
Technical/scientific	

	Work Environment
Primarily indoors	
Primarily multiple locations	

	Minimum Education Level
High school diploma	

	Salary Range
$20,200 to $32,700 to $54,800	

	Certification or Licensing
Voluntary	

	Outlook
Faster than the average	

Overview

Packaging machinery technicians work with automated machinery that packages products into bottles, cans, bags, boxes, cartons, and other containers. The machines perform various operations, such as forming, filling, closing, labeling, and marking. The systems and technologies that packaging machinery technicians work with are diverse. Depending on the job, packaging machinery technicians may work with electrical, mechanical, hydraulic, or pneumatic systems. They also may work with computerized controllers, fiber-optic transmitters, robotic units, and vision systems.

History

Packaging has been used since ancient times, when people first wrapped food in materials to protect it, or devised special carriers to transport items over long distances. One of the oldest packaging materials, glass, was used by Egyptians as early as 3000 BC. Packaging as we know it, though, has its origins in the Industrial Revolution. Machinery was used for mass production of items, and manufacturers needed some way to package products and protect them during transport. Packages and containers were developed that not only kept goods from damage during shipment, but also helped to increase the shelf life of perishable items.

Initially, packaging was done by hand. Workers at manufacturing plants hand-packed products into paper boxes, steel cans, glass jars, or other containers as they were produced. As manufacturing processes and methods improved, equipment and machines were developed to provide quicker and less expensive ways to package products. Automated machinery was in use by the 19th century and was used not only to package products but to create packaging materials. The first containers produced through automated machinery were glass containers created by Michael Owens in Toledo, Ohio, in 1903.

The use of new packaging materials, such as cellophane in the 1920s and aluminum cans in the early 1960s, required updated machinery to handle the new materials and to provide faster, more efficient production. Semiautomatic machines and eventually high-speed, fully automated machines were created to handle a wide variety of products, materials, and packaging operations. Today, packaging engineers, packaging machinery technicians, and other engineering professionals work to develop new equipment and techniques that are more time-, material-, and cost-efficient. Advanced technologies, such as robotics, are allowing for the creation of increasingly sophisticated packaging machinery.

The Job

Packaging machinery technicians work in packaging plants of various industries or in the plants of packaging machinery manufacturers. Their jobs entail building machines, installing and setting up equipment, training operators to use the equipment, maintaining equipment, troubleshooting, and repairing machines. Many of the machines today are computer-controlled and may include robotic or vision-guided applications.

Machinery builders, also called *assemblers*, assist engineers in the development and modification of new and existing machinery designs. They build different types of packaging machinery following engineering blueprints, wiring schematics, pneumatic diagrams, and plant layouts. Beginning with a machine frame that has been welded in another department, they assemble electrical circuitry, mechanical components, and fabricated items that they may have made themselves in the plant's machine shop. They may also be responsible for bolting on additional elements of the machine to the frame. After the machinery is assembled, they perform a test run to make sure it is performing according to specifications.

Field service technicians, also called *field service representatives*, are employed by packaging machinery manufacturers. They do most of their work at the plants where the packaging machinery is being used. In some companies, assemblers may serve as field service technicians; in others, the field service representative is a technician other than the assembler. In either case, they install new machinery at customers' plants and train in-plant machine operators and maintenance personnel on its operation and maintenance.

When a new machine is delivered, the field service technicians level it and anchor it to the plant floor. Then, following engineering drawings, wiring plans, and plant layouts, they install the system's electrical and electromechanical components. They also regulate the controls and setup for the size, thickness, and type of material to be processed and ensure the correct sequence of processing stages. After installation, the technicians test-run the machinery and make any necessary adjustments. Then they teach machine operators the proper operating and maintenance procedures for that piece of equipment. The entire installation process, which may take a week, is carefully documented. Field service representatives may also help the plant's in-house mechanics troubleshoot equipment already in operation, including modifying equipment for greater efficiency and safety.

Automated packaging machine mechanics, also called *maintenance technicians*, perform scheduled preventive maintenance as well as diagnose machinery problems and make repairs. Preventive maintenance is done on a regular basis following the manufacturer's guidelines in the service manual. During routine maintenance, technicians do such things as change filters in vacuum pumps, grease fittings, change oil in gearboxes, and replace worn bushings, chains, and belts. When machines do break down, maintenance technicians must work quickly to fix them so that production can resume as soon as possible. The technician might be responsible for all the machinery in the plant, one or more packaging lines, or a single machine. In a small plant, a single technician may be responsible for all the duties required to keep a packaging line running, while in a large plant a team of technicians may divide the duties.

Requirements

High School

Although a high school diploma is not required, it is preferred by most employers who hire packaging or engineering technicians. In high school, students should take geometry, and voc-tech classes such as electrical shop, machine shop, and mechanical drawing. Computer classes, including computer-aided design, are also helpful. In addition to developing mechanical and electrical abilities, students should develop communication skills through English and writing classes.

Postsecondary Training

Many employers prefer to hire technicians who have completed a two-year technical training program. Completing a machinery training program or packaging machinery program can provide students with the necessary knowledge and technical skills for this type of work. Machinery training programs can be found in community colleges, trade schools, and technical institutes throughout the country, but there are only a few technical colleges specializing in packaging machinery programs. These programs award either a degree or certificate in automated packaging machinery systems. You may get a list of these technical colleges by writing to the Packaging Machinery Manufacturers Institute.

Packaging machinery programs generally last two years and include extensive hands-on training as well as classroom study. Students may learn to use simple hand tools such as hacksaws as well as drill presses, lathes, mills, and grinders. Other technical courses cover sheet metal and welding work, power transmission, electrical and mechanical systems, maintenance operations, industrial safety, and hazardous materials handling.

Classes in packaging operations include bag making, loading, and closing; case loading; blister packaging; palletizing, conveying, and accumulating; and labeling and bar coding. There are also classes in form fill, seal wrap, and carton machines as well as packaging quality control and package design and testing. Courses especially critical in an industry where technology is increasingly sophisticated are PLC (programmable logic control), CAD/CAM (computer-aided design and manufacturing), fiber optics, robotics, and servo controls.

Certification or Licensing

Although employers may not require certification, it can provide a competitive advantage when seeking employment. A voluntary certification program is available for engineering technicians through the National Institute for Certification in Engineering Technologies (NICET). Certification is available at various levels and in different specialty fields. Most programs require passing a written exam and possessing a certain amount of work experience.

Union membership may be a requirement for some jobs, depending on union activity at a particular company. Unions are more likely found in large-scale national and international corporations. Field service technicians are usually not unionized. Maintenance technicians and assemblers may be organized by the International Brotherhood of Teamsters or the International Association of Machinists and Aerospace Workers. In addition, some technicians may be represented by the International Longshoremen's and Warehousemen's Union.

Other Requirements

Persons interested in this field should have mechanical and electrical aptitudes, manual dexterity, and the ability to work under time pressure. In addition, they should have analytical and problem solving skills. The ability to communicate effectively with people from varying backgrounds is especially important as packaging machinery technicians work closely with engineers, plant managers, customers, and machinery operators. They need to be able to listen to workers' problems as well as to explain things clearly. They frequently have to provide written reports, so good writing skills are beneficial.

Exploring

Students can test their interest for this type of work by engaging in activities that require mechanical and electrical skills, such as building a short-wave radio, taking appliances apart, and working on cars, motorcycles, and bicycles. Participating in science clubs and contests can also provide opportunities for working with electrical and mechanical equipment and building and repairing things. Taking vocational shop classes can also help students explore their interests and acquire useful skills.

Students may also visit a plant or manufacturing company to observe packaging operations and see packaging machinery technicians at work. Many plants provide school tours, and you may be able to arrange a visit through a school counselor or teacher. Reading trade publications can also familiarize students with the industry.

Employers

Packaging machinery technicians are usually employed by companies who manufacture packaging machinery or by companies who package the products they produce. Packaging is one of the largest industries in the United States so jobs are plentiful across the country; in small towns and large cities. Opportunities in the packaging field can be found in almost any company that produces and packages a product. Food, chemicals, cosmetics, electronics, pharmaceuticals, automotive parts, hardware, plastics, and almost any products you can think of need to be packaged before reaching the consumer market. Because of this diversity, jobs are not restricted to any product, geographic location, or plant size.

Starting Out

Students in a technical program may be able to get job leads through their schools' job placement services. Many jobs in packaging are unadvertised and are learned about through contacts with professionals in the industry. Students may learn about openings from teachers, school administrators, and industry contacts they acquired during training.

Applicants can also apply directly to machinery manufacturing companies or companies with manufacturing departments. Local employment offices may also list job openings. Sometimes companies hire part-time or summer help in other departments, such as the warehouse or shipping. These jobs may provide an opportunity to move into other areas of the company.

Advancement

Technicians usually begin in entry-level positions and work as part of an engineering team. They may advance from a maintenance technician to an assembler, and then move up to a supervisory position in production operations or packaging machinery. They can also become project managers and field service managers.

Workers who show an interest in their work, who learn quickly and have good technical skills, can gradually take on more responsibilities and advance to higher positions. The ability to work as part of a team and communicate well with others, plus self-motivation and the ability to work well without a lot of supervision, are all helpful traits for advancement. People who have skills as a packaging machinery technician can usually transfer those skills to engineering technician positions in other industries. Some packaging machinery technicians pursue additional education to qualify as an engineer and move into electrical engineering, mechanical engineering, packaging engineering, or industrial engineering positions. Other technicians pursue business, economics, and finance degrees and use these credentials to obtain positions in other areas of the manufacturing process, in business development, or in areas such as importing or exporting.

Earnings

Earnings vary with geographical area and the employee's skill level and specific duties and job responsibilities. Other variables that may affect salary include the size of the company and the type of industry, such as the food and beverage industry or the electronics industry. Technicians who work at companies with unions generally, but not always, earn higher salaries.

In general, technicians earn approximately $20,000 a year to start, and with experience can increase their salaries to about $33,000. Seasoned workers with two-year degrees who work for large companies may earn between $50,000 and $70,000 a year, particularly those in field service jobs or in supervisory positions.

Benefits vary and depend upon company policy, but generally include paid holidays, vacations, sick days, and medical and dental insurance. Some companies also offer tuition assistance programs, pension plans, profit sharing, and 401-K plans.

Work Environment

Packaging machinery technicians work in a variety of environments. They may work for a machinery manufacturer or in the manufacturing department of a plant or factory. Most plants are clean and well ventilated, although actual conditions vary based on the type of product manufactured and packaged. Certain types of industries and manufacturing methods can pose special problems. For example, plants involved in paperboard and paper manufacturing may have dust created from paper fibers. Workers in food plants may be exposed to strong smells from the food being processed, although most workers usually get accustomed to this. Pharmaceutical and electronic component manufacturers may require special conditions to ensure that the manufacturing environments are free from dirt, contamination, and static. Clean-air environments may be special rooms that are temperature- and moisture-controlled, and technicians may be required to wear special clothing or equipment when working in these rooms.

In general, most plants have no unusual hazards, although safety practices need to be followed when working on machinery and using tools. The work is generally not strenuous, although it does involve carrying small components and hand tools, and some bending and stretching.

Most workers work 40 hours a week, although overtime may be required, especially during the installation of new machinery or when equipment malfunctions. Some technicians may be called in during the evening or on weekends to repair machinery that has shut down production operations. Installation and testing periods of new equipment can also be very time-intensive and stressful when problems develop. Troubleshooting, diagnosing problems, and repairing equipment may involve considerable time as well as trial-and-error testing until the correct solution is determined.

Technicians who work for machinery manufacturers may be required to travel to customers' plants to install new machinery or to service or maintain existing equipment. This may require overnight stays or travel to foreign locations.

Outlook

Packaging machinery technicians are in high demand both by companies that manufacture packaging machinery and by companies that use packaging machinery. With the growth of the packaging industry, which grosses over $80 billion a year, a nationwide shortage of trained packaging technicians has developed over the last 20 years. There are far more openings than there are qualified applicants.

The packaging machinery industry is expected to continue its growth into the 21st century. American-made packaging machinery has earned a worldwide reputation for high quality and is known for its outstanding control systems and electronics. According to the Packaging Machinery Manufacturers Institute's Fourth Annual Packaging Machinery Shipments and Outlook Study, U.S. shipments of packaging machinery increased by 8.1 percent in 1997 to an estimated $4.5 billion. Continued success in global competition will remain important to the packaging machinery industry's prosperity and employment outlook.

The introduction of computers, robotics, fiber optics, and vision systems into the industry has added new skill requirements and job opportunities for packaging machinery technicians. There is already widespread application of computer-aided design and computer-aided manufacturing (CAD/CAM). The use of computers in packaging machinery will continue to increase, with computers communicating with other computers on the status of operations and providing diagnostic maintenance information and production statistics. The role of robotics, fiber optics, and electronics will also continue to expand. To be prepared for the jobs of the future, packaging machinery students should seek training in the newest technologies.

With packaging one of the largest industries in the United States, jobs can be found across the country, in small towns and large cities, in small companies or multiplant international corporations. The jobs are not restricted to any one industry or geographical location—wherever there is industry, there is some kind of packaging going on.

For More Information

The following source can provide information on educational programs, certification, and the packaging industry.

Institute of Packaging Professionals
481 Carlisle Drive
Herndon, VA 20170-4823
Tel: 703-318-8970
Email: iopp@pkgmatters.com
Web: http://www.iopp.org/

National Institute of Packaging, Handling, and Logistic Engineers
6902 Lyle Street
Lanham, MD 20706-3454
Tel: 301-459-9105
Email: niphle@erols.com
Web: http://users.erols.com/niphle/

Packaging Education Forum
481 Carlisle Drive
Herndon, VA 20170
Tel: 703-318-8975
Email: pef@pkgmatters.com
Web: http://www.packinfo-world.org/wpo/us/pef/

Packaging Machinery Manufacturers Institute
4350 North Fairfax Drive, Suite 600
Arlington, VA 22203
Tel: 703-205-0923
Web: http://www.packexpo.com

Plastics Technicians

Chemistry **Mathematics**	School Subjects
Mechanical/manipulative **Technical/scientific**	Personal Skills
Primarily indoors **Primarily one location**	Work Environment
High school diploma **Apprenticeship**	Minimum Education Level
$16,000 to $31,000 to $39,500	Salary Range
Voluntary	Certification or Licensing
Much faster than the average	Outlook

Overview

Plastics technicians are skilled professionals who help design engineers, scientists, research groups, and manufacturers develop, manufacture, and market plastics products.

Most commonly, plastics technicians work in research and development or manufacturing. In these settings, they function at a level between the engineer or scientist in charge of a job, and the production or laboratory workers who carry out most of the tasks. Other plastics technicians handle mold and tool making, materials and machinery, sales and services, and related technical tasks.

History

The plastics industry traces its commercial beginnings to 1869. A billiard ball manufacturer in New York offered a prize of $10,000 to anyone who could create an alternative material to ivory for the production of their billiard balls

(balls had been made from elephant tusks, which grew increasingly rare and expensive to obtain). A printer named John Wesley Hyatt experimented with a mixture of cellulose nitrate and camphor, creating what he called celluloid. Although he didn't win the prize, his invention, patented in 1872, brought about a revolution in production and manufacturing. By 1892, over 2,500 articles were being produced from celluloid. Among these inventions were piano keys, false teeth, the first movie film, frames for eyeglasses, flexible windows, and, of course, billiard balls. Celluloid did have its drawbacks. It could not be molded and was highly flammable.

In the years that followed, many tried to overcome these shortcomings. In 1909, Leo Hendrik Baekeland developed phenolic plastic. This product replaced natural rubber in electrical insulation, and was used for pot handles, phone handsets, chemical ware, and automobile distributor caps and rotors, and it is still used today. Other plastics materials were developed steadily. The greatest variety of materials and applications, however, came during World War II, when the war effort accelerated major changes in transportation, clothing, military equipment, and consumer goods.

Today, plastics manufacturing is a major industry whose products play a vital role in many other industries and activities around the world, including the electronics, aerospace, medical, and housing industries. According to the Society of the Plastics Industry, the U.S. plastics industry employs 1.3 million workers and provides $274 billion in annual shipments. Plastic is used in the production of computers, radar equipment, modern aircraft, medical tubing, food packaging, plumbing, paint and adhesives, home appliances, and thousands of other items. The position of plastics technician is relatively new in the industrial workforce. It was created by technological developments in the plastics industry that required people with some technical background, but not an engineering degree.

The Job

The duties of plastics technicians can be grouped into five general categories: research and development, mold and tool making, manufacturing, sales and service, and related technical tasks. In research and development, technicians work in laboratories to create new materials or to improve existing ones. In the laboratory, technicians monitor chemical reactions, test, evaluate test results, keep records, and submit reports. A wide variety of chemical apparatus is used. Technicians also use testing equipment to conduct standardized routine tests to determine properties of materials. They set up, calibrate, and operate devices to obtain test data for interpretation and comparison. John Haan is a Quality Control Layout Technician for a Japanese company called TRMI in Michigan. "I'm responsible for the verification of dimensions of assembled product that we ship to our customer," Haan says. "This audit is done on an annual basis of all parts that we make." The tools he uses in his job include calipers, micrometers, radius gauges, and thread gauges. "But mostly the Coordinate Measuring Machine (CMM), Optical Comparator, and granite surface plate with height gauge and dial indicator are used." Most of his career has been spent in machining of steel, cast iron, and aluminum, so he finds working with plastics to be an interesting challenge. "I have found that plastics present their own unique problems when it comes to inspecting parts," he says. "The parts are very flexible and any pressure on them seems to change their shape."

As new product designs are conceived, *research and development technicians* work on prototypes, assist in the design and manufacture of specialized tools and machinery, and monitor the manufacturing process. To be good at these tasks, plastics technicians must have a mechanical aptitude, thorough knowledge of a variety of materials, and the ability to solve problems.

Mold and tool making is a specialized division of plastics manufacturing. Plastics technicians with drafting skills are employed as mold and tool designers or as drawing detailers. They may also become involved in product design.

Technicians in plastics manufacturing work in molding, laminating, or fabricating. Molding requires the technician to install molds in production machines, establish correct molding cycles, monitor the molding process, maintain production schedules, test incoming raw materials, inspect goods in production, and ensure that the final product meets specifications.

Laminating technicians are trained to superimpose materials in a predetermined pattern. This process is used to make aircraft, aerospace and mass-transit vehicles, boats, satellites, surfboards, recreational vehicles, and furniture. Laminating entails bench work for small parts, and teamwork for large parts. A reinforced plastics item the size of a shoe box can be built by one person, while a large motorized vehicle for a Disney World ride requires the work of several technicians.

Technicians employed as *fabricators* work with plastic sheets, rods, and tubes, using equipment similar to that used in woodworking. Aircraft windshields and canopies, solariums, counter displays, computer housings, signs, and furniture are some of the products made by fabricators. Basic machine shop methods combined with heat-forming, polishing, and bonding are skills used by technicians in this area.

Sales and service work encompasses a wide variety of jobs for plastics technicians. These technicians are needed in the sales departments of materials suppliers, machinery manufacturers, molding companies, laminators, and fabricators.

Sales representatives for materials suppliers help customers select the correct grade of plastic. They provide a liaison between the customer and the company, assist in product and mold design, and solve problems that may arise in manufacturing.

Sales representatives for machinery manufacturers help customers select the proper equipment for their needs. *Sales technicians* are able to apply scientific training to arrive at the best selection. They are familiar with hydraulic systems and electrical circuitry in the machines they sell, and are knowledgeable about the customer's manufacturing processes.

Molding companies employ technicians to contact customers that require plastics products. Technicians help them choose the correct plastic for the job, discuss the best design, determine the optimum mold size for cost-effectiveness, and provide follow-up services.

Technicians employed in sales capacities by laminators call on the United States Air Force, Navy, Army, and Coast Guard, as well as aircraft companies and commercial businesses. They constantly update their specialized knowledge and training to keep up with the rapid technological advances in this field.

Plastics technicians are also important and valued employees in certain related fields. For example, companies that make computers, appliances, electronic devices, aircraft, and other products that incorporate plastics components rely heavily on plastics technicians to specify, design, purchase, and integrate plastics in the manufacture of the company's major product line.

Requirements

High School

A high school diploma is the minimum educational requirement for a career as a plastics technician, but this will only qualify applicants for the most basic positions. While in high school, you should take subjects designated as college preparatory. These subjects will provide a solid foundation for the specialized knowledge required of a plastics technician. Courses should include mathematics, including one year each of algebra, geometry, and trigonometry, and courses in the laboratory sciences, preferably organic chemistry and physics. English and speech classes will also help you to hone your communications skills. Mechanical drawing and shop will also be useful.

Postsecondary Training

While still in high school, you should investigate programs offered by community colleges, technical institutes, and vocational-technical schools. Some schools include plastics courses as part of mechanical or chemical technicians programs. Also, an increasing number of colleges offer bachelor's degrees in plastics technology.

A typical two-year curriculum for plastics technicians at a community college includes class, laboratory, and, sometimes, work experience. In the first year, courses typically include introduction to plastics, applied mathematics, compression molding procedures, fabrication of plastics, properties of thermo-plastics, injection molding, and extrusion molding.

Second-year courses typically include reinforced plastics procedures, applied chemistry of plastic materials, dies and molds, thermo-forming, synthetic elastomers, foamed plastics procedures, test procedures, and basic employment information.

Another training option for students is to participate in apprenticeship programs or in-plant training programs while earning a degree. Many companies operate on a three-shift basis; hours can be arranged around students' class schedules. As part of the learning experience, it is possible to participate in cooperative education or work-study programs. This is a joint venture between the school and the industry where students can work a limited number of hours per month and often receive college credit.

Students who plan to enter the military should investigate branches of service that offer training in plastics. The United States Air Force, Navy, Coast Guard, and Army publish procurement specifications, operate repair facilities, and carry on their own research and development.

In the plastics industry, each process requires a specific knowledge. For example, injection molding skills are completely different from those required for laminating. The technician who specializes in compression molding has skills not common to other processes. Certain bodies of knowledge, however, are common to all areas of the plastics industry.

Certification and Licensing

Certification isn't required of plastics technicians, but is available through the Society of the Plastics Industry (SPI). As industry equipment becomes more complex, employers may prefer to hire only certified technicians. To become an NCP Certified Operator, you'll take an exam in one of four areas: blow molding, extrusion, injection molding, or thermoforming. The exam is open to anyone seeking a career in the plastics industry, but you'll likely need at least two years plastics experience to pass the exam.

Other Requirements

You should have good hand-eye coordination and manual dexterity to perform a variety of tasks, especially building laminated structures. You must have normal eyesight; color blindness could be a limitation for those whose work requires color matching or keen color perception. You should also have good communications skills since you must interact with a variety of coworkers including various engineers, chemists, supervisors, designers, estimators, and other technicians. You must be able to follow both oral and written instructions in order to be able to create a product according to precise specifications and demands.

"I try to be organized in my work," Haan says, "doing inspections with the same set-up as much as possible, and not reinventing the wheel each time."

The hearing-impaired and those with physical handicaps perform well in areas of research and development, testing, quality control, mold and product design, inspection, and in some production and assembly departments, as well as in sales.

Exploring

Films about plastics can be obtained free of charge directly from the materials or machinery manufacturers, from lending libraries, and from professional organizations within the industry.

Through your high school counselor, you can arrange visits to community colleges, vocational-technical schools, and universities that offer technical programs. Tours of laboratories, shops, and classrooms can provide firsthand information on the nature of the courses. Part-time or summer employment at a plastics-production factory is also an option.

Employers

Primary plastics producers employ the majority of plastics technicians. A smaller number of technicians will find employment with manufacturers who have in-house plastics departments. Some major employers of plastics technicians in the United States include DuPont, Monsanto, and General

Motors. In Canada, most plastics employers are located in Ontario, Quebec, British Columbia, and Alberta.

Starting Out

Personnel managers maintain contact with schools that have ongoing plastics programs. Recruiting agents visit graduating technicians to acquaint them with current opportunities.

Experts in various fields are regularly invited to lecture at technical schools and colleges. Their advice and information can provide good ideas about finding entry-level employment.

Student chapters of the Society of Plastics Engineers maintain close ties with the parent organization. Student members receive newsletters and technical journals, and they attend professional seminars. These contacts are invaluable when seeking employment.

Field trips are an important part of the technician's education. Visits to plants and laboratories give students a broad overview of the many manufacturing processes. During these tours, students can observe working conditions and discuss employment possibilities.

Advancement

There are excellent opportunities for advancement for well-prepared technicians. Some manufacturers conduct in-plant training programs, and many provide incentives for technicians to continue their education at accredited schools. An employee with sales or customer service potential is trained in various manufacturing aspects before joining the sales or service division. Those with advanced education may become involved in supervisory or management capacities, quality control, purchasing, or cost estimating. Others may become owners of a plastic manufacturing enterprise. Technicians who are especially creative may work hand in hand with customers as designers of products and molds, or as plastics engineers.

Advancement within a company is earned by demonstrating increased technical skill or supervisory ability, together with a willingness to accept added responsibility. In molding plants, technicians advance to positions as supervisors, department heads, assistant managers, and managers. Laboratory technicians advance to positions as supervisors and managers. In the field of reinforced plastics, advanced positions are shop supervisors, quality control supervisors, and training supervisors.

Some of the other positions to which technicians can advance are described as follows:

Product designers create designs for products to be produced from plastics materials. They investigate the practicability of designs in relation to the limitations of plant equipment, cost, probable selling price, and industry specifications. *Plastics engineers* engage in the manufacture, fabrication, and use of existing materials, as well as the development of new materials, processes, and equipment.

Production managers direct the work of various production departments, either directly or through subordinate supervisors. They provide information on new production methods and equipment, problems, and the need for maintenance of all plant machinery and equipment. Production managers work closely with union representatives. *Research and development department managers* direct research studies in the development of new products and manufacturing methods. They are usually in charge of specialized testing and analytical services and of test methods to evaluate conformance to national standards.

Purchasing agents are responsible for overall direction and coordination of buyers who secure raw materials, components, packaging material, office equipment, supplies, machinery, and services for a production complex.

Earnings

According to 1997 wage surveys conducted by SPI, machine operators in the plastics industry earn between $16,000 and $22,000 a year. Quality assurance inspectors make around $21,000 a year. Computer-aided design (CAD) specialists earn between $31,000 and $39,500 a year.

Benefits often include paid vacations, health and dental insurance, pension plans, credit union services, production bonuses, stock options, and industry-sponsored education. These benefits will vary with the size and nature of the company.

Work Environment

Working conditions that technicians encounter in the plastics field vary greatly. Research or test laboratories are clean, quiet, air-conditioned, and well lighted. Normal business hours are usually observed, although some overtime may be necessary. Some companies operate more than one shift. No more than normal physical strength is required for most of the work in this profession. High safety standards are uniformly observed. Equipment is well maintained to prevent accidents to machine operators. Cleanliness in the workplace is mandatory.

Injection-molding plants are quiet to moderately noisy. Extrusion plants are quiet, clean, and efficient. Machine-heating zones are protected and product take-off or wind-up devices are guarded. Laminating procedures range from clean to extremely messy. Catalysts, solvents, and resins present hazards unless strict precautionary measures are taken to prevent accidents. Compression-molding shops are quiet, safe places to work. Temperatures during the summer can be uncomfortable; molds must be maintained at 300 degrees Fahrenheit.

Plastics technicians are key employees in many enterprises. Such positions are rewarding from both a financial and psychological viewpoint. "It is very satisfying to know that I am somewhat in control of the quality of the product we produce," Haan says. "Also, we get to see things that will be on cars and trucks in the future. I get to interact with the engineering staff and have input into what goes on."

Outlook

The plastics industry encompasses so many employment categories that employment is virtually assured for any qualified graduate of a technical program. Worldwide expansion of this industry is expected to continue through 2008. This expansion is expected to create a strong demand for technicians who can meet the challenges of this changing industry. Those who pursue advanced education and who acquire a variety of skills and talents will have the best employment opportunities. More plastics technicians will be needed because of the increasing focus on cheaper and more effective ways of recycling and making other types of plastics biodegradable. Other jobs will arise from the automobile industry changing over many of its metal parts to plastics.

For More Information

For a career brochure and information about education and certification, contact:

Society of the Plastics Industry
1801 K Street, NW, Suite 600K
Washington, DC 20006-1301
Tel: 202-974-5200
Web: http://www.plasticsindustry.org/

The APC is a trade industry that offers a great deal of information about the plastics industry, and maintains an informative Web site:

American Plastics Council (APC)
1300 Wilson Boulevard, Suite 800
Arlington, VA 22209
Tel: 800-2-HELP-90
Web: http://www.plastics.org

For information about scholarships, seminars, and training, contact:

Plastics Institute of America
University of Massachusetts-Lowell
333 Aiken Street
Lowell, MA 01854
Tel: 978-934-3130
Web: http://www.eng.uml.edu/Dept/PIA/public_html/

For information on student membership, contact:

Society of Plastics Engineers
PO Box 403
Brookfield, CT 06804-0403
Tel: 203-775-0471
Web: http://www.4spe.org

Radiation Protection Technicians

Mathematics Physics	School Subjects
Mechanical/manipulative Technical/scientific	Personal Skills
Indoors and outdoors Primarily one location	Work Environment
Associate's degree	Minimum Education Level
$25,000 to $33,000 to $42,000	Salary Range
None available	Certification or Licensing
About as fast as the average	Outlook

Overview

Radiation protection technicians monitor radiation levels, protect workers, and decontaminate radioactive areas. They work under the supervision of nuclear scientists, engineers, or power plant managers and are trained in the applications of nuclear and radiation physics to detect, measure, and identify different kinds of nuclear radiation. They know federal regulations and permissible levels of radiation.

History

All forms of energy have the potential to endanger life and property if allowed to get out of control. This potential existed with the most primitive uses of fire, and it exists in the applications of nuclear power. Special care must be taken to prevent uncontrolled radiation in and around nuclear power plants. Skilled nuclear power plant technicians are among the workers who monitor and control radiation levels.

Around 1900, scientists discovered that certain elements give off invisible rays of energy. These elements are said to be radioactive, which means that they emit radiation. Antoine-Henri Becquerel (1852-1908), Marie Curie (1867-1934), and Pierre Curie (1859-1906) discovered and described chemical radiation before the turn of the century. In 1910, Marie Curie isolated pure radium, the most radioactive natural element, and in 1911 she was awarded the Nobel Prize for Chemistry for her work related to radiation.

Scientists eventually came to understand that radiation has existed in nature since the beginning of time, not only in specific elements on earth, such as uranium, but also in the form of cosmic rays from outer space. All parts of the earth are constantly bombarded by a certain background level of radiation, which is considered normal or tolerable.

During the 20th century, research into the nature of radiation led to many controlled applications of radioactivity, ranging from X rays to nuclear weapons. One of the most significant of these applications, which has impacted our everyday life, is the use of nuclear fuel to produce energy. Nuclear power reactors produce heat that is used to generate electricity.

The biological effects of radiation exposure continue to be studied, but we know that short-term effects include nausea, hemorrhaging, and fatigue; long-range and more dangerous effects include cancer, lowered fertility, and possible birth defects. These factors have made it absolutely clear that if radiation energy is to be used for any purpose, the entire process must be controlled. Thus, appropriate methods of radiation protection and monitoring have been developed; it is the radiation protection technician's job to insure that these methods are accurately and consistently employed.

The Job

The work of radiation protection technicians is to protect workers, the general public, and the environment from overexposure to radiation. Many of their activities are highly technical in nature: they measure radiation and radioactivity levels in work areas and in the environment by collecting samples of air, water, soil, plants, and other materials; record test results and inform the appropriate personnel when tests reveal deviations from acceptable levels; help power plant workers set up equipment that automatically monitors processes within the plant and records deviations from established radiation limits; and calibrate and maintain such equipment using hand tools.

Radiation protection technicians work efficiently with people of different technical backgrounds. They instruct operations personnel in making the necessary adjustments to correct problems such as excessive radiation levels, discharges of radionuclide materials above acceptable levels, or improper chemical levels. They also prepare reports for supervisory and regulatory agencies.

Radiation protection technicians are concerned with "ionizing radiation," particularly three types known by the Greek letters alpha, beta, and gamma. Ionization occurs when atoms split and produce charged particles. If these particles strike the cells in the body, they cause damage by upsetting well-ordered chemical processes.

In addition to understanding the nature and effects of radiation, technicians working in nuclear power plants also know the principles of nuclear power plant systems. They have a thorough knowledge of the instrumentation that is used to monitor radiation in every part of the plant and its immediate surroundings. They also play an important role in educating other workers about radiation monitoring and control.

Radiation protection technicians deal with three basic radiation concepts: time, distance from the radiation source, and shielding. When considering time, technicians know that certain radioactive materials break down into stable elements in a matter of days or even minutes. Other materials, however, continue to emit radioactive particles for thousands of years. Radiation becomes less intense in proportion to its distance from the source, so distance is an important concept in controlling radiation exposure. Shielding is used to protect people from radiation exposure and appropriate materials with a specific thickness needed to be used to block emission of radioactive particles.

Because radiation generally cannot be seen, heard, or felt, radiation protection technicians use special instruments to detect and measure it and to determine the extent of radiation exposure. Technicians use devices that measure the ionizing effect of radiation on matter to determine the presence of radiation and, depending on the instrument used, the degree of radiation danger in a given situation.

Two such devices are Geiger counters and dosimeters, which measure received radiation doses. Dosimeters are often in the form of photographic badges worn by personnel and visitors. These badges are able to detect radioactivity because it shows up on photographic film. Radiation protection technicians calculate the amount of time that personnel may safely work in contaminated areas, considering maximum radiation exposure limits and the radiation level in the particular area. They also use specialized equipment to detect and analyze radiation levels and chemical imbalances.

Finally, although the radiation that is released into the environment surrounding a nuclear facility is generally far less than that released through background radiation sources, radiation protection technicians must be prepared to monitor people and environments during abnormal situations and emergencies.

Under normal working conditions, technicians monitor the work force, the plant, and the nearby environment for radioactive contamination; test plant workers for radiation exposure, both internally and externally; train personnel in the proper use of monitoring and safety equipment; help *nuclear materials handling technicians* prepare and monitor radioactive waste shipments; perform basic radiation orientation training; take radiation contamination and control surveys, air sample surveys, and radiation level surveys; maintain and calibrate radiation detection instruments using standard samples to determine accuracy; ensure that radiation protection regulations, standards, and procedures are followed and records kept of all regular measurements and radioactivity tests; and carry out decontamination procedures that ensure the safety of plant workers and the continued operation of the plant.

Requirements

High School

Prospective technicians should have a solid background in basic high school mathematics and science. Courses should include four years of English, at least two years of mathematics including algebra, and at least one year of physical science, preferably physics with laboratory instruction. Computer programming and applications, vocational machine shop operations, and blueprint reading also provide a good foundation for further studies.

Postsecondary Training

After high school, the prospective technician should study at a two-year technical school or community college. Several public or private technical colleges offer programs designed to prepare nuclear power plant radiation protection technicians. Other programs, called nuclear technology or nuclear materials handling technology, also provide a good foundation. You should be prepared to spend from one to two years in postsecondary technical training taking courses in chemistry, physics, laboratory procedures, and technical writing. Because the job entails accurately recording important data and writing clear, concise technical reports, technicians need excellent writing skills.

A typical first year of study for radiation protection technicians includes introduction to nuclear technology, radiation physics, mathematics, electricity and electronics, technical communications, radiation detection and measurement, inorganic chemistry, radiation protection, blueprint reading, quality assurance/quality control, nuclear systems, computer applications, and radiation biology.

Coursework in the second year includes technical writing, advanced radiation protection, applied nuclear chemistry, radiological emergencies, advanced chemistry, radiation shielding, radiation monitoring techniques, advanced radionuclide analysis, occupational safety and health, nuclear systems and safety, radioactive materials disposal and management, and industrial economics.

Students who graduate from nuclear technician programs are usually hired by nuclear power plants or other companies and institutions involved in nuclear-related activities. These employers provide a general orientation to their operations and further training specific to their procedures.

Certification or Licensing

At present, there are no special requirements for licensing or certification of nuclear power plant radiation protection technicians. Some graduates of radiation control technology programs, however, may want to become nuclear materials handling technicians. For this job, licensing may be required, but the employer usually will arrange for the special study needed to pass the licensing test.

Other Requirements

Federal security clearances are required for workers in jobs that involve national security. Nuclear Regulatory Commission (NRC) clearance is required for both government and private industry employees in securing related positions. Certain projects may necessitate military clearance with or without NRC clearance. Employers usually help arrange such clearances.

Exploring

Vocational guidance counselors are valuable resources for high school students interested in this occupation. Students also can obtain information from the occupational information centers and their staff at community and technical colleges.

High school science classes may be the best places to gain familiarity with the nature of this career. Science teachers may be able to arrange field trips and invite speakers to describe various careers. Nuclear reactor facilities are unlikely to provide tours, but they may be able to furnish literature on radiation physics and radiation control. Radiation protection technicians employed at nuclear-related facilities may be invited to speak about their chosen field.

Radiation is used for medical diagnosis and treatment in hospitals all over the country. Radiology departments of local hospitals often provide speakers for science or career classes.

In addition, a utilities company with a nuclear-fired plant may be able to offer a tour of the visitor's center at the plant, where much interesting and valuable information about nuclear power plant operation is available. Small reactors used for experiments, usually affiliated with universities and research centers, also may give tours.

Employers

Radiation protection technicians are employed by government agencies, such as the Department of Energy and the Department of Defense as well as electric power utilities that operate nuclear plants. Other than utilities, technicians are employed by nuclear materials handling and processing facilities, regulatory agencies, nondestructive testing firms, radiopharmaceutical industries, nuclear waste handling facilities, nuclear service firms, and national research laboratories.

Starting Out

The best way to enter this career is to graduate from a radiation control technology program. Another excellent way to enter the career is to join the United States Navy and enter its technical training program for various nuclear specialties.

Graduates of radiation control technology programs are usually interviewed and recruited while in school by representatives of companies with nuclear facilities. At that time, they may be hired with arrangements made to begin work soon after graduation. Graduates from strong programs may receive several attractive job offers.

Entry-level jobs for graduate radiation protection technicians include the position of *radiation monitor*. This position involves working in personnel monitoring, decontamination, and area monitoring and reporting. Another entry-level job is *instrument calibration technician*. These technicians test instrument reliability, maintain standard sources, and adjust and calibrate instruments. *Accelerator safety technicians* evaluate nuclear accelerator operating procedures and shielding to ensure personnel safety. *Radiobiology technicians* test the external and internal effects of radiation in plants and animals, collect data on facilities where potential human exposure to radiation exists, and recommend improvements in techniques or facilities.

Hot-cell operators conduct experimental design and performance tests involving materials of very high radioactivity. *Environmental survey technicians* gather and prepare radioactive samples from air, water, and food specimens. They may handle nonradioactive test specimens for test comparisons with National Environmental Policy Act standards. *Reactor safety technicians* study personnel safety through the analysis of reactor procedures and shielding and through analysis of radioactivity tests.

Advancement

A variety of positions is available for experienced and well-trained radiation protection technicians. *Research technicians* develop new ideas and techniques in the radiation and nuclear field. *Instrument design technicians* design and prepare specifications and tests for use in advanced radiation instrumentation. *Customer service specialists* work in sales, installation, modification, and maintenance of customers' radiation control equipment. *Radiochemistry technicians* prepare and analyze new and old compounds, utilizing the latest equipment and techniques. *Health physics technicians* train new radiation monitors, analyze existing procedures, and conduct tests of experimental design and radiation safety. *Soils evaluation technicians* assess soil density, radioactivity, and moisture content to determine sources of unusually high levels of radioactivity. *Radioactive waste analysts* develop waste disposal techniques, inventory stored waste, and prepare waste for disposal.

Some of the most attractive opportunities for experienced radiation protection technicians include working as radiation experts for a company or laboratory, or acting as consultants. Consultants may work for nuclear engineering or nuclear industry consulting firms or manage their own consulting businesses.

Earnings

The earnings of radiation protection technicians who are beginning their careers depend on what radiation safety program they work in (nuclear power, federal or state agencies, research laboratories, medical facilities, etc.). They may begin as salaried staff or be paid hourly wages. Technicians who receive hourly wages usually work in shifts and receive premium pay for overtime.

Trained technicians earn annual salaries of up to $25,000 a year. After three to five years of experience, they can expect to earn as much as $33,000 a year. Consultants may earn as much as $42,000 a year. Earnings are also affected by whether technicians remain in their entry-level jobs or become supervisors and whether they are able to pass a national competency test that makes them a Nationally Registered Radiation Protection Technologist.

Technicians usually receive benefits, such as paid holidays and vacations, insurance plans, and retirement plans. Because of the rapid changes that occur in the radiation safety industry, many employers pay for job-related study and participation in workshops, seminars, and conferences.

Work Environment

Depending on the employer, work environments vary from offices and control rooms to relatively cramped and cold areas of power plants.

Of all power plant employees, radiation protection technicians are perhaps best able to evaluate and protect against the radiation hazards that are an occupational risk of this field. The safety of all plant workers depends on the quality and accuracy of their work.

Radiation protection technicians wear film badges or carry pocket monitors to measure their exposure to radiation. Like all other nuclear power plant employees, technicians wear safety clothing, and radiation-resistant clothing may be required in some areas. This type of clothing contains materials that reduce the level of radiation before it reaches the human body.

In some of the work done by radiation protection technicians, radiation shielding materials, such as lead and concrete, are used to enclose radioactive materials while the technician manipulates these materials from outside the contaminated area. These procedures are called hot-cell operations. In some areas, automatic alarm systems are used to warn of radiation hazards so that proper protection can be maintained.

The career of a radiation protection technician is very demanding. Technicians must have confidence in their ability to measure and manage potentially dangerous radioactivity on a daily basis. Radiation protection technicians play an important teaching role in the nuclear energy-fueled power plant. They must know the control measures required for every employee and be capable of explaining the reasons for such measures. Because abnormal conditions sometimes develop in the nuclear power industry, technicians must be able to withstand the stress, work long hours without making mistakes, and participate as a cooperating member of a team of experts.

Successful technicians are usually individuals who are able to confidently accept responsibility, communicate effectively in person and on paper, and enjoy doing precise work. Their participation is vital to the successful application of nuclear technology.

Outlook

At the end of the 1990s, there were 110 nuclear power plants licensed to operate in 32 of the United States. However, there are no orders for new nuclear power plants to be built, and several have begun plans to permanently shut down and become decommissioned. Consequently, the total number of plants in the United States will begin to decrease in the foreseeable future.

Even if the nuclear power industry experiences a decline, the employment outlook for radiation protection technicians should remain strong. Technicians are needed to support radiation safety programs in Department of Energy facilities, Department of Defense facilities, hospitals, universities, state regulatory programs, federal regulatory agencies, and many industrial activities. New technicians will be needed to replace retiring technicians or technicians who leave the field for other reasons. Increased efforts to enforce and improve safety standards may also result in new jobs for technicians. Because radiation programs have been in development for half a century, most of the radiation safety programs are well-established and rely primarily on technicians to keep them running.

For More Information

This nonprofit, international, scientific, educational organization provides career information, publications, scholarships, and seminars and cooperates in educational efforts.

American Nuclear Society
555 North Kensington Avenue
LaGrange Park, IL 60526
Tel: 708-352-6611
Web: http://www.ans.org

This professional organization of more than 6,000 members promotes the practice of radiation safety. Society activities include encouraging research and radiation science, developing standards, and disseminating radiation safety information.

Health Physics Society
1313 Dolley Madison Boulevard, Suite 402
McLean, VA 22101
Tel: 703-790-1745
Email: HPS@BurkInc.com
Web: http://www.hps.org

This organization is dedicated to the peaceful use of nuclear technologies. Its 300 members provide a strong voice in matters of national energy policy. Visit their Web site to access, Careers and Education: Your Bright Future in Nuclear Energy and Technology.

Nuclear Energy Institute
1776 I Street, NW, Suite 400
Washington, DC 20006-3708
Tel: 202-739-8000
Web: http://www.nei.org/

Semiconductor Technicians

School Subjects
Chemistry
Mathematics
Physics

Personal Skills
Communication/ideas
Technical/scientific

Work Environment
Primarily indoors
Primarily one location

Minimum Education Level
Associate's degree

Salary Range
$25,000 to $43,750 to $62,000

Certification or Licensing
Voluntary

Outlook
Much faster than the average

Overview

Semiconductor technicians are highly skilled workers who test new kinds of semiconductor devices being designed for use in many kinds of modern electronic equipment. They may also test samples of devices already in production to assess production techniques. Moreover, they help develop and evaluate the test equipment used to gather information about the semiconductor devices. Working under the direction provided by engineers in research laboratory settings, they assist in the design and planning for later production or help to improve production yields. There are close to 250,000 technicians employed in the United States in the semiconductor industry. Those identified as semiconductor technicians account for 63,000 of those jobs, according to the U.S. Bureau of Labor Statistics.

History

Semiconductors and devices utilizing them are found in nearly every electronic product made today, from complicated weapons systems and space technology, to personal computers, video cassette recorders, and programmable coffee makers. The manufacturing of semiconductors and microelectronics devices requires the efforts of a variety of people, from the engineers who design them, to the technicians who process, construct, and test them.

Although the word semiconductor is often used to refer to microchips or integrated circuits, a semiconductor is actually the basic material of these devices. Semiconductor materials are so titled because they can be treated to act with properties between that of an insulator, which does not conduct electrical current, and that of a true conductor of electrical current, such as metal.

Silicon is the most common material used as a semiconductor. Other semiconductor materials may be gallium arsenide, cadmium sulfide, and selenium sulfide. Doping, or treating, these materials with substances such as aluminum, arsenic, boron, and phosphorous gives them conducting properties. By applying these substances according to a specifically designed layout, engineers and technicians construct the tiny electronic devices—transistors, capacitors, and resistors—of an integrated circuit. A microchip no larger than a fingernail may contain many thousands of these devices.

The Job

There are many steps that occur in processing semiconductors into integrated circuits. The technicians involved in these processes are called semiconductor development technicians and semiconductor process technicians. They may be involved in several or many of the steps of semiconductor manufacturing, depending on where they work. Often, semiconductor technicians function as a link between the engineering staff and the production staff in the large-scale manufacturing of semiconductor products.

The making of semiconductors begins with silicon. To be used, the silicon must be extremely pure. The silicon used for semiconductors is heated in a furnace and formed into cylinder rods between one and six inches in diameter, and three or more feet in length. These rods are smoothed and polished until they are perfectly round, and then sliced into wafers of between one-quarter and one-half millimeter in thickness. Then the wafers are processed, by etching, polishing, heat-treating, and lapping, to produce the desired dimensions and surface finish. After the wafers are tested, measured, and inspected for any defects, they are coated with a photosensitive substance called a photoresist.

The engineering staff and the technicians assigned to assist them prepare designs for the layout of the microchip. This work is generally done using a computer-aided design (CAD) system. The large, completed design is then miniaturized as a photomask when it is applied to the wafer. The photomask is placed over the wafer and the photoresist is developed, much like film in a camera, with ultraviolet light, so that the layout of the microchip is reproduced many times on the same wafer. This work takes place in a specially equipped clean room, or laboratory, kept completely free of dust and other impurities. During the miniaturization process, the tiniest speck of dust will ruin the reproduction of the layout on the wafer.

Next, the wafer is doped with the substances that will give it the necessary conducting properties. Technicians follow the layout, like a road map, when adding these substances. The proper combinations of materials create the various components of the integrated circuit. When this process is complete, the wafer is tested by computerized equipment that can test the many thousands of components in a matter of seconds. Many of the integrated circuits on the wafer will not function properly, and these are marked and discarded. After testing, the wafer is cut up into its individual chips.

The chips are then packaged by placing them in a casing usually made of plastic or ceramic, which also contains metal leads for connecting the microchip into the electronic circuitry of the device for which it will be used. It is this package that people usually refer to as a chip or semiconductor.

Semiconductor process technicians are generally responsible for the fabrication and processing of the semiconductor wafer. *Semiconductor development technicians* usually assist with the basic design and development of rough sketches of a prototype chip; they may be involved in transferring the layout to the wafer and in assembling and testing the semiconductor. Both types of technicians gather and evaluate data on the semiconductor, wafer, or chip. They are responsible for making certain that each step of the process precisely meets test specifications, and also for identifying flaws and problems in the material and design. Technicians may also assist in designing and building new test equipment, and in communicating test data and production instructions for large-scale manufacture. Technicians may also be responsible for maintaining the equipment and for training operators on its use.

Requirements

The nature of the microelectronics industry, where technological advances are continuous and rapid, means that some form of higher education, whether in a two-year or four-year program, is a must. An early interest in and excitement for electronics and computers is a good indicator of someone who might be interested in this career.

High School

Math and science courses, as well as classes in computers and computer science, are obvious requirements for students wishing to enter the semiconductor and microelectronics field. Physics and chemistry will be helpful for understanding many of the processes involved in developing and fabricating semiconductors and semiconductor components. Strong communications skills are also very important.

Postsecondary Training

Technician jobs in microelectronics and semiconductor technology require at least an associate's degree in electronics or electrical engineering or technology. Students may attend a two-year program at a community college or vocational school. Students interested in a career at the engineering level should consider studying for a bachelor's degree. The trend toward greater specialization within the industry may make a bachelor's degree more desirable over an associate's degree in the future.

An electronics engineering program will include courses in electronics theory, as well as math, science, and English courses. Students can expect to study such subjects as the principle and models of semiconductor devices; physics for solid state electronics; solid state theory; introduction to VLSI systems; and basic courses in computer organization, electromagnetic fundamentals, digital and analog laboratories, and the design of circuits and active networks. Companies will also provide additional training on the specific equipment and software they use. Many companies also offer training programs and educational opportunities to employees to increase their skills and their responsibilities.

Courses are available at many community and junior colleges, which may be more flexible in their curriculum, and better able to keep up with technological advances than vocational training schools. The latter, however, will often have programs geared specifically to the needs of the employers in their area, and may have job placement programs and relationships with the different companies available as well. If you are interested in these schools, you should do some research to determine whether the training offered is thorough, and that the school has a good placement record. Training institutes should also be accredited by the National Association of Trade and Technical Schools.

Military service will also provide a strong background in electronics. In addition, the tuition credits available to military personnel will be helpful when continuing your education.

Certification or Licensing

Certification is not mandatory, but voluntary certification may prove useful in locating work, and in increasing your pay and responsibilities. The International Society of Certified Electronics Technicians (ISCET) offers certification testing at various levels and fields of electronics. The ISCET also offers a variety of study and training material to help prepare for the certification tests.

Other Requirements

A thorough understanding of semiconductors, electronics, and the production process is necessary for semiconductor technicians. Investigative and research skills, and a basic knowledge of computers and computer programs are also important skills for the prospective semiconductor technician. "You have to be very patient and not easily discouraged to work in this industry," says Jan Gilliam, a semiconductor technician at Advanced Micro Devices, located in Austin, Texas. "You have to really focus on the goal while paying close attention to details."

Exploring

You can develop your own interest in computers and microelectronics while in school. Because of the rapid advances in electronics technology, most high schools will be unable to keep up, and you will need to read and explore on your own. Joining extracurricular clubs in computers or electronics will give you an opportunity for hands-on learning experiences.

You should also begin to seek out the higher education appropriate for your future career interests. Your high school guidance counselor should be able to help you find a training program that will match your career goals.

Employers

Finding a job in the semiconductor industry may mean living in the right part of the country. Certain states, such as California, Texas, and Massachusetts, have many more opportunities than others do. Some of the big names in semiconductors are Intel, Motorola, Texas Instruments, and National Semiconductor. These companies are very large and employ many technicians, but there are smaller and mid-size companies in the industry as well.

Starting Out

Semiconductor technician positions can be located through the job placement office of a community college or vocational training school. Since an associate's degree is recommended, many of these degree programs provide students with job interviews and introductions to companies in the community who are looking for qualified workers.

Job listings in the newspaper or at local employment agencies are also good places for locating job opportunities. Aspiring semiconductor technicians can also find lower-skilled positions in the semiconductor industry and work hard for promotion to a technician position. The huge market for semiconductors and the devices related to them means that many job opportunities are available to qualified people.

Advancement

As with any manufacturing industry, the advancement possibilities available to semiconductor technicians will depend on their levels of skill, education, and experience. Technicians may advance to senior technicians or may find themselves in supervisory or management positions. Technicians with two-year associate's degrees may elect to continue their education. Often, their coursework will be transferable to a four-year engineering program, and many times their employer may help pay for their continuing education. Semiconductor technicians may ultimately choose to enter the engineering and design phases of the field. Also, a background in semiconductor processing and development may lead to a career in sales or purchasing of semiconductor components, materials, and equipment.

Earnings

Because of the stringent requirements, qualified semiconductor technicians command salaries which tend to be higher than many other professions. According to a 1998 salary survey by *Circuits Magazine*, the average technician with a two-year degree earned $43,750, with starting salaries at about $25,000 and upper salaries of $62,000. Technicians earning the higher salaries have more education and have worked in the industry for many years.

Work Environment

The work of semiconductor technicians is not physically strenuous and is usually done in an extremely clean environment. Technicians may work with hazardous chemicals, however, and proper safety precautions must be strictly followed. Because of the large demand for semiconductors and related devices, many facilities, like Advanced Micro Devices, where Gilliam works, operate with two 12-hour shifts, meaning that a technician may be assigned to the night or weekend shift, or on a rotating schedule. Gilliam works for three days and then is off for four.

Because of the need for an extremely clean environment, technicians are required to wear clean-suits to keep dust, lint, and dirt out of the clean room where the production takes place.

An important component in most manufacturing processes is the speed with which products are produced. Workers may find themselves under a great deal of pressure to maintain a certain level of production volume. The ability to work well in a sometimes stressful environment is an important quality for any prospective semiconductor technician.

Outlook

The semiconductor industry is expected to remain a strong source of employment into the next century. The increasing demand for semiconductors and related devices in most areas of industry, manufacturing, and consumer services will mean the steady need for personnel trained in their development and processing. New applications for semiconductor technology are continually being created, and these too will spur the demand for trained technical staff. Advancements in technology will require increased and continuing educational requirements for persons seeking and holding positions in this industry.

For More Information

For certification information, contact:

International Society of Certified Electronics Technicians
2708 West Berry Street
Fort Worth, TX 76109-2356
Tel: 817-921-9101
Web: http://www.iscet.org/

For industry information and educational programs, contact:

Semiconductor Equipment and Materials International
805 East Middlefield Road
Mountain View, CA 94043-4080
Tel: 605-964-5111
Email: semihq@semi.org
Web: http://www.semi.org/

For industry information, contact:

Semiconductor Industry Association
181 Metro Drive, Suite 450
San Jose, CA 95110
Tel: 408-436-6600
Web: http://www.semichips.org/

SEMATECH, a non-profit research and development consortium of U.S. semiconductor manufacturers, sponsors the Discover a New World of Opportunity Web site. Visit the site to get information on careers, associate's degree and certification programs, and profiles of workers in the field. Additionally, the site has a FAQ section and a Glossary of semiconductor industry terms:

Discover a New World of Opportunity
http://www.4chipjobs.com/index.html

Wastewater Treatment Plant Operators and Technicians

School Subjects
Chemistry
Mathematics

Personal Skills
Mechanical/manipulative
Technical/scientific

Work Environment
Indoors and outdoors
Primarily one location

Minimum Education Level
Some postsecondary training

Salary Range
$18,000 to $29,660 to $55,000

Certification or Licensing
Required by certain states

Outlook
About as fast as the average

Overview

Wastewater treatment plant operators control, monitor, and maintain the equipment and treatment processes in wastewater (sewage) treatment plants. They remove or make harmless the chemicals, solid materials, and organisms in wastewater so that the water is not polluted when it is returned to the environment. Wastewater treatment plant technicians work under the supervision of wastewater treatment plant operators. Technicians take samples and monitor treatment to ensure treated water is safe for its intended use. Depending on the level of treatment, water is used for human consumption or for nonconsumptive purposes, such as field irrigation or discharge into natural water sources. Some technicians also work in labs where they collect and analyze water samples and maintain lab equipment.

History

Water systems and the disposal of wastes are ancient concerns. Thousands of years ago, the Minoans on the island of Crete built some of the earliest known domestic drainage systems. Later, the Romans created marvelous feats of engineering, including enclosed sewer lines that drained both rain runoff and water from the public baths. Urban sanitation methods, however, were limited. Garbage and human wastes were collected from streets and homes and dumped into open watercourses leading away from the cities.

These processes changed little until the 19th century. The health hazards of contact with refuse were poorly understood, but as populations grew, disease outbreaks and noxious conditions in crowded areas made sanitation an important issue. Problems worsened with the Industrial Revolution, which led to both increased population concentrations and industrial wastes that required disposal.

Early efforts by sanitation engineers in the 19th century attempted to take advantage of natural processes. Moderate amounts of pollutants in flowing water go through a natural purification that gradually renders them less harmful. Operators of modern wastewater treatment plants monitor the process that does essentially the same thing that occurs naturally in rivers to purify water, only faster and more effectively. Today's plants are highly sophisticated, complex operations that may utilize biological processes, filtration, chemical treatments, and other methods of removing waste that otherwise may allow bacteria to colonize (live in) critical drinking supplies.

Wastewater treatment operators and technicians must comply with stringent government standards for removing pollutants. Under the Federal Water Pollution Control Act of 1972 and later reauthorizations, it is illegal to discharge any pollutant into the environment without a permit. Industries that send wastes to municipal treatment plants must meet minimum standards and pretreat the wastes so they do not damage the treatment facilities. Standards are also imposed on the treatment plants, controlling the quality of the water they discharge into rivers, streams, and the ocean.

The Job

Wastewater from homes, public buildings, and industrial plants is transported through sewer pipes to treatment plants. The wastes include both organic and inorganic substances, some of which may be highly toxic, such as lead and mercury. Wastewater treatment plant operators and technicians regulate the flow of incoming wastewater by adjusting pumps, valves, and other equipment, either manually or through remote controls. They keep track of the various meters and gauges that monitor the purification processes and indicate how the equipment is operating. Using the information from these instruments, they control the pumps, engines, and generators that move the untreated water through the processes of filtration, settling, aeration, and sludge digestion. They also operate chemical-feeding devices, collect water samples, and perform laboratory tests, so that the proper level of chemicals, such as chlorine, is maintained in the wastewater. Technicians may record instrument readings and other information in logs of plant operations. These logs are supervised and monitored by operators. Computers are commonly used to monitor and regulate wastewater treatment equipment and processes. Specialized software allows operators to store and analyze data, which is particularly useful when something in the system malfunctions.

The duties of operators and technicians vary somewhat with the size and type of plant where they work. In small plants one person per shift may be able to do all the necessary routine tasks. But in larger plants, there may be a number of operators, each specializing in just a few activities and working as part of a team that includes engineers, chemists, technicians, mechanics, helpers, and other employees. Some facilities are equipped to handle both wastewater treatment and treatment of the clean water supplied to municipal water systems, and plant operators may be involved with both functions.

Other routine tasks that plant operators and technicians perform include maintenance and minor repairs on equipment such as valves and pumps. They may use common hand tools such as wrenches and pliers and special tools adapted specifically for the equipment. In large facilities, they also direct attendants and helpers who take care of some routine tasks and maintenance work. The accumulated residues of wastes from the water must be removed from the plant, and operators may dispose of these materials. Some of this final product, or sludge, can be reclaimed for uses such as soil conditioners or fuel for the production of electricity.

Technicians may also survey streams and study basin areas to determine water availability. To assist the engineers they work with, technicians prepare graphs, tables, sketches, and diagrams to illustrate survey data. They file plans and documents, answer public inquiries, help train new personnel and perform various other support duties.

Plant operators and technicians sometimes have to work under emergency conditions, such as when heavy rains flood the sewer pipes, straining the treatment plant's capacity or when there is a chlorine gas leak or oxygen deficiency in the treatment tanks. When a serious problem arises, they must work quickly and effectively to solve it as soon as possible.

Requirements

High School

A high school diploma or its equivalent is required for a job as a wastewater treatment plant operator or technician, and additional specialized technical training is generally preferred for both positions. A desirable background for this work includes high school courses in chemistry, biology, mathematics, and computers; welding or electrical training may be helpful as well. Other characteristics that employers look for are mechanical aptitude and the ability to perform mathematical computations easily. You should be able to work basic algebra and statistics problems. Future technicians may be required to prepare reports containing statistics and other scientific documentation. Communications, statistics, and algebra are useful for this career path: such courses enable the technician to prepare graphs, tables, sketches, and diagrams to illustrate surveys for the operators and engineers they support.

Postsecondary Training

As treatment plants become more technologically complex, workers who have previous training in the field are increasingly at an advantage. Specialized education in wastewater technology is available in two-year programs that lead to an associate's degree and one-year programs that lead to a certificate. Such programs, which are offered at some community and junior colleges and vocational-technical institutes, provide a good general knowledge of water pollution control and will prepare you to become an operator or technician. Beginners must still learn the details of operations at the plant where they work, but their specialized training increases their chances for better positions and later promotions.

Many operators and technicians acquire the skills they need during a period of on-the-job training. Newly hired workers often begin as attendants or operators-in-training. Working under the supervision of experienced operators, they pick up knowledge and skills by observing other workers and by doing routine tasks such as recording meter readings, collecting samples, and general cleaning and plant maintenance. In larger plants, trainees may study supplementary written material provided at the plant or they may attend classes where they learn plant operations.

Wastewater treatment plant operators and technicians often have various opportunities to continue learning about their field. Most state water pollution control agencies offer training courses for people employed in the field.

Subjects covered by these training courses include principles of treatment processes and process control, odors and their control, safety, chlorination, sedimentation, biological oxidation, sludge treatment and disposal, and flow measurements. Correspondence courses on related subject areas also are available. Some employers help pay tuition for workers who take related college-level courses in science or engineering.

Certification or Licensing

In most states, workers who control operations at wastewater treatment plants must be certified by the state. To obtain certification, operators must pass an examination given by the state. There is no nationwide standard, so different states administer different tests. Many states issue several classes of certification, depending on the size of the plant the worker is qualified to control. Certification may be beneficial even if it is not a requirement and no matter how much experience a worker already has. In Illinois, for example, operators who have the minimum state certification level are automatically eligible for higher pay than those without any certification, although certification is not a requirement of hire.

Other Requirements

Operators and technicians must be familiar with the provisions of the Federal Clean Water Act and various state and local regulations that apply to their work. Whenever they become responsible for more complex processes and equipment, they must become acquainted with a wider scope of guidelines and regulations. In larger cities and towns especially, job applicants may have to take a civil service exam or other tests that assess their aptitudes and abilities.

Exploring

It may be possible to arrange to visit a wastewater treatment plant to observe its operations. It can also be helpful to investigate courses and requirements of any programs in wastewater technology or environmental resources programs offered by a local technical school or college. While part-time or summer employment as a helper in a wastewater treatment plant could be a very helpful experience, such a job may be hard to find. However, a job in any kind of machine shop can provide an opportunity to become familiar with handling machinery and common tools.

Asking wastewater plant operators or technicians in your city if you can interview them about their job is a good way to learn about the job, and it may help you fulfill a requirement for a class paper or speech. Learning about water conservation and water quality in general can also be useful. Government agencies or citizen groups dedicated to improving water quality or conserving water can teach you about water quality and supply in your area.

Employers

While municipal wastewater treatment plants employ the majority of wastewater treatment professionals, there are other employers who need workers skilled in this field. Wastewater treatment plant operators and technicians may also find jobs for state or federal water pollution control agencies, monitoring plants, and providing technical assistance. Examples of such agencies are the Army Corps of Engineers and the Environmental Protection Agency. These jobs normally require vocational-technical school or community college training. Other experienced wastewater workers find employment with industrial wastewater treatment plants, companies that sell wastewater treatment equipment and chemicals, large utilities, consulting firms, or vocational-technical schools.

Starting Out

Graduates of most postsecondary technical programs and some high schools can get help in locating job openings from the placement office of the school they attended. Another source of information is the local office of the state employment service. Job seekers may also directly contact state and local water pollution control agencies and the personnel offices of wastewater treatment facilities in desired locations.

In some plants, a person must first work as a wastewater treatment plant technician before becoming an operator or working in a supervisory position. Wastewater treatment plant technicians have many of the same duties as a plant operator, but less responsibility. They inspect, study, and sample existing water treatment systems and evaluate new structures for efficacy and safety. Support work and instrumentation reading make up the bulk of the technician's day.

The Internet has become a useful resource for finding job leads. Professional associations, such as the Water Environment Foundation, offer job listings in the wastewater field as part of their Web site (http://www.wef.org). Such Web sites are a good place for someone getting started in the field as they also list internship or trainee positions available. Also, an Internet search using the words "wastewater treatment plant operator, or technician" will generate a list of sites that may contain job postings and internship opportunities.

Advancement

As operators gain skills and experience, they are assigned tasks that involve more responsibility for more complex activities. Some technicians advance to become operators. Some operators advance to become plant supervisors or plant superintendents. The qualifications that superintendents need are related to the size and complexity of the plant. In smaller plants, experienced operators with some postsecondary training may be promoted to superintendent positions. In larger plants, educational requirements are increasing along with the sophistication and complexity of their systems, and superintendents usually have bachelor's degrees in engineering or science.

For some operators and technicians, the route to advancement is transferring to a related job. Such jobs may require additional schooling or training to specialize in water pollution control, commercial wastewater equipment sales, or teaching wastewater treatment in a vocational or technical school.

Earnings

Salaries of wastewater treatment plant operators and technicians vary depending on factors such as the size of the plant, the workers' job responsibilities, and their level of certification. According to the *Occupational Outlook Handbook*, entry-level plant technicians can expect to make at least $18,000 per year. Water and liquid waste treatment plant operators earned median annual salaries of $29,660 in 1998. The lowest 10 percent earned

$18,500 or less, while the highest 10 percent earned $44,710 or more a year. Experienced certified workers can make over $55,000 depending on the size of the plant and staff they supervise. In addition to their pay, most operators and technicians receive benefits such as life and health insurance, a pension plan, and reimbursement for education and training related to their job.

Work Environment

Most of the approximately 98,000 wastewater treatment plant operators in the United States are employed by local governments; others work for the federal government, utility companies, or private sanitary services that operate under contracts with local governments. Jobs are located throughout the country, with the greatest numbers found in areas with high populations. In small towns, plant operators may only work part time or may handle other duties as well as wastewater treatment. The size and type of plant also determine the range of duties. In larger plants with many employees, operators and technicians usually perform more specialized functions. In some cases, they may be responsible for monitoring only a single process. In smaller plants, workers likely will have a broader range of responsibilities. Wastewater treatment plants operate 24 hours a day, every day of the year. Operators and technicians usually work one of three eight-hour shifts, often on a rotating basis so that employees share the evening and night work. Overtime is often required during emergencies.

The work takes operators and technicians both indoors and outdoors. They must contend with noisy machinery and may have to tolerate unpleasant odors, despite the use of chlorine and other chemicals to control odors. The job involves moving about, stooping, reaching, and climbing. Operators and technicians often get their clothes dirty. Slippery sidewalks, dangerous gases, and malfunctioning equipment are potential hazards on the job, but by following safety guidelines, workers can minimize their risk of injury.

Outlook

Through 2008, employment in this field is expected to grow as fast as the average for all occupations. The growth in demand for wastewater treatment will be related to the overall growth of the nation's population and economy. New treatment plants will probably be built, and existing ones will be upgraded, requiring additional trained personnel to manage their operations. Other openings will arise when experienced workers retire or transfer to new occupations. Operators and technicians with formal training will have the best chances for new positions and promotions.

Workers in wastewater treatment plants are rarely laid off, even during a recession, because wastewater treatment is essential to public health and welfare. In the future, more wastewater professionals will probably be employed by private companies that contract to manage treatment plants for local governments.

For More Information

For current information on the field of wastewater management, contact:

American Water Works Association
6666 West Quincy Avenue
Denver, CO 80235
Tel: 303-794-7711
Web: http://www.awwa.org

For information on education and training, contact:

Coalition of Environmental Training Centers
2930 East Camelback Road, Suite 185
Phoenix, AZ 85016
Tel: 602-956-6099

Environmental Careers Organization
179 South Street
Boston, MA 02111
Tel: 617-426-4375
Web: http://www.eco.org

The following is a professional organization monitoring developments in the field of wastewater management. Visit their Web site to access their Careers in Water Quality *brochure and other career information:*

Water Environment Federation
601 Wythe Street
Alexandria, VA 22314-1994
Tel: 800-666-0206
Web: http://www.wef.org

Welding Technicians

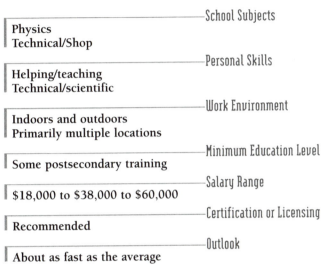

	School Subjects
Physics Technical/Shop	
	Personal Skills
Helping/teaching Technical/scientific	
	Work Environment
Indoors and outdoors Primarily multiple locations	
	Minimum Education Level
Some postsecondary training	
	Salary Range
$18,000 to $38,000 to $60,000	
	Certification or Licensing
Recommended	
	Outlook
About as fast as the average	

Overview

Welding technicians are the link between the welder and the engineer and work to improve a wide variety of welding processes. As part of their duties, they may supervise, inspect, and find applications for the welding processes. Some technicians work in research facilities where they help engineers test and evaluate newly developed welding equipment, metals, and alloys. When new equipment is being developed or old equipment improved, they conduct experiments on it, evaluate the data, then make recommendations to engineers. Other welding technicians, who work in the field, inspect welded joints and conduct tests to ensure that welds meet company standards, national code requirements, and customer job specifications. These technicians record the results, prepare and submit reports to welding engineers, and conduct welding personnel certification tests according to national code requirements.

History

The origins of modern welding reach back thousands of years. Archaeological evidence suggests that primitive forms of welding were known even in prehistoric times. Ancient Egyptians practiced a form of welding similar to our gas welding in which they used a blowpipe and a flame from burning alcohol to heat the metal surfaces to be welded.

During the 19th century, new methods for joining two pieces of metal were developed, and existing methods were refined. Resistance welding was developed in 1857. In this method, the metal parts to be joined are pressed together and a surge of electrical current is sent through the metal at the point of contact. The combination of pressure and heat formed by electrical resistance results in the formation of a solid welded nugget that holds the pieces of metal together. This method was not perfected until 1886 because of the lack of sufficient electrical power.

Thermite welding, which fuses two pieces of metal by means of thermite (a mixture of aluminum and iron oxide), was first used in 1898. Arc welding, a process of fusing metal by means of heat generated from an electrical arc, was developed experimentally in 1881 and was first used commercially in 1889.

Gas welding uses the heat of burning gas, such as a mixture of acetylene and oxygen. Although oxygen was identified in 1774 and acetylene in 1836, the effect of joining the two gases was not discovered until 1895, when improved methods of commercial production of acetylene and oxygen were developed. The year 1903 marked the beginning of the commercial use of the oxyacetylene process in welding and cutting.

During the 20th century, these methods were further improved and dozens of new methods developed. Two other methods now commonly used are brazing and induction welding. In brazing, a filler metal is heated along with the metal surfaces and flows into a specially prepared joint. Induction welding uses an induction coil that generates heat and is very efficient for certain shapes such as small-diameter, thin-walled steel tubing.

The Job

The welding technician is the link between the welder and the engineer or production manager. Welding technicians fill positions as supervisors, inspectors, experimental technicians, sales technicians, assistants to welding engineers, and welding analysts and estimators.

Some beginning welding technicians are employed as *welding operators*. They perform manual, automatic, or semiautomatic welding jobs. They set up work, read blueprints and welding-control symbols, and follow specifications set up for a welded product.

As *welding inspectors*, welding technicians judge the quality of incoming materials, such as electrodes, and of welding work being done. They accept or reject pieces of work according to required standards set forth in codes and specifications. A welding inspector must be able to read blueprints, interpret requirements, and have a knowledge of testing equipment and methods.

Closely related to this work is that of the *welding qualification technician*. This person keeps records of certified welders and supervises tests for the qualification of welding operators.

Other welding technicians work as *welding process-control technicians*. These technicians set up the procedures for welders to follow in various production jobs. They specify welding techniques, types of filler wire to be used, ranges for welding electrodes, and time estimates. Welding technicians also provide instructions concerning welding symbols on blueprints, use of jigs and fixtures, and inspection of products.

Equipment maintenance and sales technicians work out of welding supply houses. They set up equipment sold by their company, train welding operators to use it, and troubleshoot for customers.

Welding technicians may also work as *technical writers*. In this position, they work closely with professional staff members to prepare reports and develop articles for technical or professional publications. Welding technicians may also work for in-house publications or trade magazines.

After more years of experience, welding technicians may be employed as welding analysts and estimators, welding engineering assistants, or welding equipment or product salespeople. *Welding analysts and estimators* analyze all the factors involved in a job, such as labor, material, and overhead, to determine what it will cost. *Welding engineering assistants* test welded metal parts, analyze design differences for a variety of welded structures, and determine welding's effects on a variety of metals. Some senior welding technicians may eventually advance in their companies to positions as welding supervisors, welding instructors, and welding production managers.

Requirements

High School

Interested high school students should have a good background in English, mathematics, physics, and chemistry. Courses that teach composition and communications skills are particularly important to the prospective technician. Shop courses also will prove helpful.

Postsecondary Training

Most prospective welding technicians should plan to complete a two-year associate's degree program. The U.S. Armed Forces also provide a welding technician training program.

Students with a concentration in welding technology should take comprehensive courses in welding practice or theory. They also need at least one course in applied physics—covering mechanics, heat, light, elementary electricity, materials, and metallurgy—to understand metals common in industry; basic metal production and fabrication techniques; and the structures, physical and chemical properties, and uses of metals.

Welding technicians should understand lattice structure, alloy systems, mechanical tests, and characteristics of strength, elasticity, ductility, malleability, and heat treatment. Elementary chemistry, which relates to metallurgy, is usually covered in metallurgical class and laboratory study.

Another area of training helpful to the welding technician is a course in metal shaping, forming, and machine-shop practice. Knowledge of drilling, tapping, reaming, shaping, and lathe and mill operation is useful. In addition, welding technicians should have some training in electronics. They may be called upon to read an electrical wiring diagram for a particular piece of equipment or to check the voltage on a machine. Courses in nondestructive testing also are helpful for the prospective welding technician.

Certification or Licensing

Welding technicians may qualify for certification as engineering technicians. In addition, they may be certified under any of the many certification programs conducted for welders; however, certification is usually not required for technicians who do not perform actual production welding.

Other Requirements

Welding technicians should enjoy working with their hands and doing research. They must be able to use drawing instruments and gauges, perform laboratory tests, and supervise and control machinery and test equipment. They are also required to collect data and assemble it into written reports. Because welding technicians work with management as well as with production personnel, they must have a sense of responsibility and the ability to get along with people.

Exploring

To observe welders or welding technicians at work, you may arrange to take field trips to manufacturing companies that use various welding processes to get an overall view of working conditions and the type of work performed.

Employers

Employment for welding technicians can be found in practically any industry: aircraft, appliances, armaments, automobiles, food processing plants, nuclear energy, radio, railroads, shipbuilding, structural engineering, and television.

Starting Out

Graduates of accredited engineering technology programs seldom have problems finding employment. Employers usually keep in close contact with these schools and often hire able students before graduation. Most graduates of two-year welding technician programs enter industry as welding operators or as assistants to welding engineers or welding production managers. This experience forms the foundation for future problem solving and job growth, allowing the graduate technician to apply both practice and theory.

Advancement

With experience, welding technicians become eligible for higher-paying jobs. Those who advance fastest have displayed a sense of personal initiative, especially in attending courses, seminars, and technical meetings that help broaden their knowledge and prepare them for more responsible positions.

With higher-paying jobs come greater responsibilities. Some welding technicians, for instance, become welding supervisors and take on the responsibility for assigning jobs to workers and showing them how the tasks should be performed. They must supervise job performance and ensure that operations are performed correctly and economically. Other technicians become welding instructors, teaching welding theory, techniques, and related processes. Finally, some technicians advance to the position of welding production manager, responsible for all aspects of welding production: equipment, materials, process control, inspection, and cost control.

Earnings

The salary range for welding technicians varies according to the individual's function and level of education as well as the geographical location of the business. In general, however, starting salaries for welding technicians who are graduates of post-high school technical programs average $18,000 to $20,000 per year in industry. Salaries will increase with experience. Most graduates of technical or other recognized institutions offering technical training earn salaries that range from $24,400 to $30,400 per year after five years on the job. Those welding technicians in research and development earn an average of $48,000, while section heads earn between $58,000 and $60,000.

Work Environment

Welding technicians are employed by a variety of industries, ranging from aircraft manufacturers to heavy-equipment plants. Working conditions vary from performing tests in clean, well-lighted research and testing laboratories to laying pipeline in the extreme heat of the desert or the cold of Alaska.

In both training and responsibility, welding technicians occupy a position between the professionally trained scientist or engineer and the skilled trades worker. Although no position carries with it the promise of complete happiness, many welding technicians have found that this position offers them status and security, steady employment, and the opportunity to travel.

Outlook

There is an increasing variety of jobs open to welding technicians in industry. This is due to the great number of new inventions and technical processes that use an even wider variety of metals, alloys, and nonmetallic materials that can be joined by welding processes.

Most welding technicians work in industrial production settings; therefore, the actual number of welding technicians employed will be influenced by economic conditions. Anticipated modest industrial expansion through 2008, and increasingly complex modern technology might mean more demand for all kinds of engineering technicians, including welding technicians. This is especially true for those who search for and develop new and technically advanced products, equipment, and procedures.

The diversity of industries in which welding technicians work helps cushion them against threats to employment caused by economic downturns for a particular industry. If economic conditions, and hence employment opportunities, become unfavorable in one industry, there remain others that require the welding technician's training and experience.

For More Information

For information on welding careers and the free video, Welding: So Hot, It's Cool, *contact:*

American Welding Society
550 NW LeJeune Road
Miami, FL 33126
Tel: 800-443-9353
Web: http://www.aws.org/

Index